HEART OF MALENESS

HEART OF MALENESS

An Exploration

Raphaël Liogier

Translated from the French by Antony Shugaar

OTHER PRESS / NEW YORK

Library of Congress Cataloging-in-Publication Data

Names: Liogier, Raphaël, author. | Shugaar, Antony, translator.
Title: Heart of maleness / Raphaël Liogier ; translated from French
by Antony Shugaar.
Other titles: Descente au cœur du mâle. English
Description: New York : Other Press, [2020] | "Originally published in French,
2018"—Title page verso. | Includes bibliographical references.
Identifiers: LCCN 2019033329 (print) | LCCN 2019033330 (ebook) |
ISBN 9781635429930 (Trade Paperback) | ISBN 9781635429947 (ebook)
Subjects: LCSH: Sex role in the work environment. | Male domination
(Social structure) | Social control. | Patriarchy. | Pay equity. |
Sex discrimination against women.
Classification: LCC HD6060.6 .L57 2020 (print) | LCC HD6060.6 (ebook) |
DDC 305.3—dc23
LC record available at https://lccn.loc.gov/2019033329
LC ebook record available at https://lccn.loc.gov/2019033330

"No one is more arrogant toward women, more aggressive or scornful, than the man who is anxious about his virility."

—SIMONE DE BEAUVOIR, *The Second Sex*

"In fine, there's nothing so sweet as to triumph over the resistance of a fair one; I share in this the ambition of famous conquerors who fly forever from victory to victory and cannot resolve to set bounds to their desires."

—MOLIÈRE, *Don Juan*

"Woman as an allegedly natural being is a product of history, which denatures her."

—THEODOR ADORNO, MAX HORKHEIMER, *Dialectic of Enlightenment*

CONTENTS

THE BANALITY OF MALENESS 3

THE PROBLEM IS DON JUAN 8

FIVE WAYS TO UNDERMINE THE
MEANING OF #METOO 12

THE TRANSCENDENTAL VALUE
OF CONSENT 24

WHAT THE MYTH OF PRINCE
CHARMING TELLS US 27

WOMAN AS CAPITAL 29

THE PRICE OF WOMEN 33

GIRLS GET IN FREE 37

VIRILITY IS TRANSMITTED
THROUGH WOMEN 39

WOMAN, INCOMPLETE IN BODY AND SOUL 43

RAPE CULTURE 47

THE IMPOTENCE OF VIRILITY 51

THE ANGUISH OF FEMALE OVERKILL 56

THE WOMAN WHO CAN HAVE
ENDLESS ORGASMS   59

THE CULTURE OF IMPOTENCE   62

ESCAPING FROM THE GILDED CAGE   66

THE UNKEPT PROMISE OF MODERNITY   68

THE FALSE AMBIGUITY OF
FEMALE CONSENT   72

SEX WITHOUT LOVE   76

GENDER MALAISE   80

DON'T FEAR THE FREEDOM   85

PLAYING WITH OUR DIFFERENCES   88

TOWARD PEACE BETWEEN THE GENDERS   92

EPILOGUE: TRANSVALUATION   95

Notes   99

Bibliography   103

HEART OF MALENESS

When I sat down to write this book, aghast at the stories countless women were posting with the hashtag #MeToo, I had a moment of doubt. Because I am a heterosexual, white, affluent, Western man, a citizen of the European Union, in short, supposedly immune to discrimination, I was afraid that anything I might say would lack legitimacy. At least, that is, if I was trying to produce anything more than distant musings, arm's-length observations; at least, if I hoped to achieve any sort of full personal engagement with this issue. In time, though, my doubts subsided: there was no need for me to talk about women at all—their singular nature, their essence. In any case, I wouldn't have known how. What I needed to conjure up, instead, was the world that we all share, a world in which a stunning inequality stubbornly persists, even now, an imbalance subtly fed by our common perceptions and our everyday behavior. In that case, it was enough to be human, really, to be able to claim legitimacy. To think otherwise, to believe that some dark veil could forever divide feminine from masculine—to believe in a mysterious and unbridgeable difference—would have betrayed the very meaning of what I was sitting down to write.

As I ventured deeper into the accounts of sexual harassment and even rape that women had been providing since October 2017, I felt a surge of disgust. The disgust gradually turned into dismay. These men are revolting, no doubt about it. Often, pathetic. Many are shameless pigs. Above all, though, they're men just like me. And it is the very fact that they are men that makes them pigs. Even if I was unwilling to accept it then and there, a part of my identity as a man had just been thrown into my face. It would be pure hypocrisy to deny it. Even if I had no distinct acts of harassment on my conscience, I could see, emerging vaguely in the background of these stark depictions of grim tableaux, the ways in which I myself had long been conditioned to view and desire women. I make no claim to any new gender theory, much less do I intend to lecture about feminism. But really, if I stop to think about it, I'm speaking mainly *to* men. For that matter, I'm basically writing *about* them, too. I'm addressing them *as* a man, and I'm writing about my own problem. Because I'm convinced that, above and beyond all the media hype, women today have clearer ideas about themselves than "we" do. At least when it comes to what they do want and what they don't. In contrast, behind an increasingly fragile façade, my fellow men are having a hard time accepting the collapse of their empire of virility, a decline and fall that is unmistakably heralded by the worldwide impetus and power of #MeToo. They are struggling, I am struggling, *we* are struggling to redefine our ambitions as men, our fantasies as men, our behavior as men, our desires as men. In short, our place in the world. Our relations with women. Our identity. Even if most of us know perfectly well that we have no choice but to change.

THE BANALITY OF MALENESS

The stunning arrest of Dominique Strauss-Kahn at New York's JFK airport on May 14, 2011, as he was about to board a flight to Europe, did not bring with it any larger debate about the Situation of Women. And yet the whole business resulted in a worldwide media storm. The case involved a powerful man accused of sexual assault on a woman who was dependent on him—much like what happened in the Weinstein case, six years later. *He*, the accused man, was the managing director of the International Monetary Fund at the time and a sure bet for future president of the French Republic. *She*, the alleged victim, was a young Guinean maid working at the Manhattan hotel where he was staying. It emerged in the aftermath of his arrest that the man was a perpetually randy sexual predator. He was forced out of his executive perch at the IMF and was effectively ruled out as a potential presidential candidate back in France. But he dragged down no other men in his calamitous fall. There was no domino effect. There were certainly other women, their claims suddenly cast in a far more credible light, who brought their own descriptions of the appalling behavior to which he'd subjected them. Our eyes were suddenly opened to DSK as a sexual glutton, a libertine pig, a diseased lothario. He was depicted as unhinged. In a word, an abnormal individual.

The producer and movie tycoon Harvey Weinstein was also spectacularly toppled from his pedestal—reviled by Hollywood en masse—in the wake of a strongly accusatory article in the October 5, 2017, issue of the *New York Times*. His fall, however, resulted in an explosive chain reaction. Because here, with repercussions that went well beyond the individual actions of an isolated predator—however monstrous—we were suddenly presented with the larger system we live in, revealed in the harsh light of day. The fundamentally unfair rules of our modern civilization were now illuminated by the pitiless light cast by the personal accounts offered by millions of women. Why this sudden tsunami? Why this surge of scandals in every walk of life, with resignations of cabinet ministers and members of parliament, expulsions of college professors, and firings of business executives across the face of the globe? Unquestionably kairos played its part—sheer chance, contingent circumstance, simple opportunity. The election to the White House of an aging playboy oozing virility to a degree that verged on the burlesque, an impulsive and proven harasser, also surely played a part. We should remember that, in the fall of 2016, in the thick of the American presidential campaign, it was hard to give serious credence to this buffoonish uber-male parading through the mass media like the circus come to town. He appeared to the eyes of the world a little bit like one of the last living exemplars of a species on the verge of extinction. And yet: Donald Trump was elected president of the United States. There was no denying it: in brutal defiance of the belief system of the progressive elites, the archaic world of the alpha male—dominant to the point of caricature—with his meek and picture-perfect "trophy wife" at his side (these are Trump's own words),[1] still existed and was, in fact, in a state of rude good health.

The seismic fault, at the very heart of society, between the old world of glorious virility, on the one hand, and—on the other—the ideological maturity reinforced by the economic autonomy women had attained was becoming increasingly and unmistakably hard to ignore. And therefore, all the more intolerable.

Beginning in the middle of the twentieth century, in fact, a growing number of women had challenged the limitations intrinsic to their status as second-class citizens, managing to climb to positions that made them equal to men, if not actually to supplant them. First in the realms of school and higher education, and then, in the course of time and in the face of resistance that endures to the present day, in the professional and political worlds. These women did nothing more than take modernity at face value. Still, there has been a growing gap between women's aspirations to acquire the means of earning a living in accordance with the modern principles of equality, on the one hand, and the persistent, die-hard resistance, and even resurgence of male behaviors which deny them that equality in everyday life. The culture of patriarchy in its most abject manifestations, radiating an aura of bad faith, has become all the more intolerable as an ever deeper moat has been dug to thwart women's real-world ambitions. Lest we forget, the French Revolution did one big thing: it enshrined in concrete terms the aspirations of the bourgeoisie to free itself of the yoke of a corrupt aristocracy, a noble class that was already philosophically illegitimate.

Making male domination really and truly intolerable would likewise require a new and broad-based awareness resting upon long-acknowledged principles which have, nonetheless, in the real world, been flouted on a daily basis.

The film producer Harvey Weinstein became the poster child for this brand of concrete inequality of the sexes, in the face of this modern world that loudly and parodistically proclaimed gender equality. Why Weinstein in particular, rather than any other random famous serial sexual harasser plucked from the ranks of thousands, and cast in the image of the former managing director of the IMF? Because DSK represented nothing more than a randy male, in a constant, frantic quest for sex. With call girls and other prostitutes. With women who were his social equals, and women who were not. With female journalists who were there to interview him, with office assistants, secretaries, housekeepers—with any woman who crossed his path. This type of behavior, of course, is a significant part of the culture of domination. But it's not its fundamental and underlying principle.

Weinstein, on the other hand, as depicted in the many eyewitness accounts, was not so much hell-bent on purchasing or procuring himself sexual services, whatever the cost and whatever the means. The rape he practiced was something more radical. He wanted the women he invited to his hotel suite—and whom he received dressed in a bathrobe, supposedly to discuss the launching or the promising continuation of their film careers—to know beyond any shadow of a doubt the real reason they were there. That they were there to submit, consciously and willingly, to him. He wanted to relish the sheer sensation of their dependency. Of their passive obedience. That is why he demanded, without the slightest rhetorical camouflage, as shamelessly as possible, that they massage him, take their clothes off, slide between the sheets with him. Not only did he not fear the gross incongruity of the situation, he actively encouraged it. One female journalist, who interviewed him before the onslaught of the impending media thunderstorm, was astonished to see that he didn't even bother to deny the charges of rape that were already starting to make the rounds. If anything, he relished his reputation. According to their own accounts, there were women who felt humiliated, defiled, unworthy of being loved, after he had sexually imposed himself upon them, and yet who not only chose *not* to report his actions to the police for years on end, but even sought out his attention, his gratitude, his friendship. They were hoping for some form of reparation, some act of kindness on the part of their torturer, in order to offset their by now abjectly debased self-image. Weinstein used women's bodies as a way of fully enjoying his power. When he succeeded in *taking possession* of them, he thrilled to the knowledge that they were offering themselves to him without desire, merely because they consciously accepted his dominance. In the far-fetched hypothesis that they took any pleasure, most likely that knowledge would only have somewhat diminished his pleasure. So he did nothing to seduce them, to assuage whatever reluctance they might have felt; quite the opposite, he always pushed things to the limits of the intolerable, he worked to humiliate them by means of his openly indecent and unashamed attitude. His enjoyment of women's bodies was a direct expression of his enjoyment of his own power. It was therefore not so much a sexual thirst he was slaking: it was really his thirst for power. He needed them in order to assert his own power. As far as he was concerned, the only will that counted was his.

THE PROBLEM IS DON JUAN

We should therefore compare DSK to Casanova. *Systematic harassment*. Whereas Weinstein can be compared to Don Juan: the *systemic* reduction of women who must consciously accept that they are nothing more than a physical object to be enjoyed, to be exploited. They are not the masters of their own selves. They cannot enjoy their own selves, therefore they cannot even take pleasure from their own bodies, by the very principle of the patriarchal system. This denial of female enjoyment can be translated—and is indeed still translated among certain groups of people—into the physical form of female genital mutilation. But it still persists to a greater or lesser degree in all societies in the implicit form of *symbolic and moral mutilation*, the very essence of which is Don Juanism. To the eye of a Don Juan, women are objects to be appropriated. To be stolen. Prey to hunt down, to trap, even to slaughter. Don Juan refuses to consider that the women he hunts and traps are human beings with desires of their own, who experience pleasure and possess free will. Otherwise known as *animate beings*. To him, they are bodies without souls. Or, perhaps, he takes pleasure in denying the existence of their souls and, thus, reducing them to their flesh. He denies the very possibility of a relationship. He takes pleasure in the degradation that he imposes upon them. He doesn't desire women. He fucks them. And so they allow him to fuck them—in his eyes and in the eyes of society at large. They are losers, because he triumphs over them. All that counts is *having* them, taking possession of them. They are *had*, then, in both senses of the word. The language expresses it clearly: when a man *has* a woman, that woman has been *had*. She is reduced to a piece of property that *can be had*. Casanovism is certainly one consequence of this unequal game. But Don Juanism is its root cause. It is even, perhaps, the first cause of male domination, something that has by no means been eliminated, even if certain of its pernicious effects have been combatted, at times with success.

Don Juan denies the existence of any free will in the women he abuses. And it is precisely this denial—the invisible principle of the unequal intimate and social game being played between men and women—that is, in the final analysis, denounced. Certainly, there have been scholarly papers and collective feminist protests that clearly perceived the issues at stake, but never before has there been a peaceful insurrection of this scope and expanse. After centuries of beating around the bush, of denunciations of inequality and the glass ceiling and gaps in pay at equal levels of professional qualification, harangues against the exclusion of women from the armed forces, the sciences, the halls of thought, art, and politics, even from the very history of humanity, the #MeToo movement and its various national affiliates are finally aiming at the very *heart of maleness.* I hope my reader will forgive me for a play on words that is not as frivolous as it might once have seemed: because it is certainly *maleness—mâlitude,* we might say in French— culturally constructed over the millennia, passing itself off as natural, biological, intellectual, self-evident, that is the problem—again, in French, *le mal (evil)*—not morally evil in and of itself, but a *malady,* a disease for which it is high time that human beings found a cure.

⌀⌀

This movement, in fact, hits the bull's-eye, the center of the target of inequality between men and women. Still, we should not misinterpret it. It's not an epiphenomenon that we can reduce to a passing trend "relegated" to the pages of women's magazines; not something we can rail against because we can no longer "flirt" or "pick up women" or "have a little harmless fun"; not something we can discredit because allegations leveled at will are an open door bound to lead to verdicts without proof; or something to be denounced because it is somehow an affront to the honor of men at large (by taking literally the comparison of men to pigs, and therefore mere beasts, less than human). Behind these hypocritical diatribes—hypocritical in the sense of the structural hypocrisy described by the sociologist Pierre Bourdieu, who called it the most powerful and insidious of all forms of hypocrisy—we can see the looming shape of the immense interests at stake. Political correctness is not, as certain commentators, both male and female, try to claim, on the side of the women who have finally found the courage to speak up. And in particular, to speak up as *one*, on an unprecedented scale. If you go to the trouble of carefully reading their accounts, you cannot help but be struck by the decency, the self-restraint, and indeed the responsibility that they display. You can sense a desire for disclosure and reform, but no thirst for revenge.

It is not just a major social movement that proves that the Internet can become a means of spontaneous mobilization in the public square; or even that digital globalization can allow unprecedented forms of transnational solidarity. Rather, it's a historic event: the culminating moment of the process of universal recognition of *transcendental subjectivity*. In other words, it's the accomplishment of the very program of modernity: the concrete acknowledgment, among all human beings, of an indivisible individual Will, prior and superior to all social conditioning, to all economic differences, to all ethnic distinctions, and all biological determinism. This universal recognition is the underlying foundation of subjective rights (also known as human rights), and it endows meaning to the principles of equality before the law and the inalienable nature of liberty.

Behind the multiplicity of circumstantial situations narrated on the Internet, it is the existential Situation of Women that comes to the fore. As I write these words, millions of tweets have been posted by women who have been harassed, humiliated, insulted, or raped. On a daily basis. Not as a rare exception, not as a marginal instance, no, but rather as a constant, day and night, in the privacy of the home, on the job, in the street, everywhere. But because it is the very principle of domination that is being called into question, the resistance and sidestepping is all the more virulent and insidious; and, for that matter, typical of times of great and radical change.

FIVE WAYS TO UNDERMINE THE MEANING OF #METOO

— The first way consists of focusing on the supposed injustice of destroying the lives of innocent men without any tangible proof. It means skipping over the fundamental rights to a presumption of innocence, due process, a fair trial. It entails the incessant refrain that most men aren't *pigs* (one should certainly hope not!). One must point to the sneaking suspicion that this means opening the floodgates to the fury of women spurned, or the thirst for fame of women who latch onto celebrities solely and exclusively in order to become famous themselves. Clearly, we cannot rule out the possibility that, as in any revolution, there will be some who will wrongly take advantage of circumstances. Nor can we exclude the emergence of extremists, as was the case in the French Revolution. But that is no argument against the revolution in and of itself; it's only a reminder that we must work to ensure that legal institutions do their jobs properly, taking due and deliberate note of any charges. For that matter, we should make a clear distinction between individual and collateral cases of injustice, and general and typical cases of systemic injustice. If I myself were wrongly accused of sexual harassment, I would surely consider that to be unfair. I would want to see my hypothetical accuser found guilty of perjury for her lies. But that would do nothing to discredit the general idea of accusations of harassment, even in my view. What is at stake here goes well beyond the set of men who have been or might yet be accused, whether rightly or wrongly. What is at stake is the principle that, according to social mores, a certain kind of behavior is no longer acceptable. What's more, that we must change the way we continue, even now, to think of women. For that matter, this attempt to discredit the #MeToo movement clearly demonstrates the mental laziness of its detractors, unwilling to go to the trouble of diving into the Twitter feed. If they were to do so, they would see that personal accusations are the exception, while the honest denunciation of situations experienced is the norm. So few names, so many cases of endlessly recursive sexual violence.

— Behaving as though the problem concerned only *other men* is the second way of resisting #MeToo. Certain men, therefore, can put the blame only upon those *pigs*, with whom, of course, they reject any and all comparison. As if it were solely a problem of disreputable people, individuals who are sexist by nature, and not a larger problem with society itself. This form of resistance, this willful insistence on turning a blind eye, can affect an entire society. As is the case in China, where many voices are raised in all seriousness to state that sexual harassment and inequality are exclusively Western problems. What then should we say about the schools for Chinese girls where they are taught to recite by heart that their first duty is to obey their husband? What then should we say about sex scandals covered up in the very heart of the highest Chinese nomenklatura? What then should we say about female infanticide in China, Korea, and India, where girls are viewed as a burden on the family? And this is not about trying to say that things are worse in Asia or in the West. It's always possible to say that things are worse here, or elsewhere. But that's still a way of chastely averting one's gaze from the all-encompassing presence of the problem, which is pretty much what has happened in France. One TV-friendly philosopher who shall remain nameless has gone so far as to declare that *all this talk* of sexual harassment simply hides the *real problem* of the infiltration of Islamists in the land of Voltaire. Always *the other*, of course, never *us*, the good Frenchmen, *les bons Français*, the good Americans, the good Westerners! In the aftermath of allegations about the sexual practices of the Muslim theologian Tariq Ramadan in late November 2017, all of France was swept by a deranged discussion of how secular culture could *never* be so repressive, about gender inequality under Islam, about the veil, and also, of course, about…terrorism. This was a textbook example of how to sidestep the matter at hand. A professor at an oral exam might understandably rap a student's knuckles for wandering off topic in this way. People pretended to forget that most of the prominent men facing allegations of sexual harassment have nothing at all to do with Islam. Among them, in France, we might well mention an ultra-charismatic and elegantly attired former president of the French Movement of Young Socialists, Thierry Marchal-Beck.

Marchal-Beck was an outspoken advocate of feminism while simultaneously harassing female members of his party, forcing some of them to give him sexual favors, sometimes just before a conference. While outwardly treating gender equality as a top priority, he was behaving like an overpowerful Don Juan, threatening his victims when they refused to submit to his desires. The disjunction between his public persona of the hypercool, progressive, and even feminist guy and his private, behind-the-curtain behavior is not unique to him, especially among powerful personalities.

But in some countries—such as France, I'm not proud to say—the typical response has been to deny the existence of the problem by placing the blame on *the Other*. The case of Marchal-Beck, who was forced out of his role in light of the scandal (albeit at the last minute, when it was impossible to do otherwise), is an exception.

By contrast, in the United Kingdom, cabinet ministers and members of parliament tender their resignations. In the United States, prominent businessmen, executives, anchormen, and television producers are shown the door. In France, nothing happens. Or in any case, very little. You can count the resignations and firings on the fingers of one hand, while they proliferate rapidly on the other side of the Channel or the Atlantic. In France, everything's fine. The only problems are with Muslims, Arabs, no doubt, the occasional Roma, certainly immigrants as a group, and perhaps the issue of strait-laced Americans. And as a result: absolutely no examination of our collective conscience. For that matter, if we really wanted to stop to think about the matter of how "we" view Muslim women in France, then we'd be forced to admit that the deranged obsession with head scarves must necessarily point to a certain element of male chauvinism. And not necessarily on the part of the "male sexist" Muslims. If anything, the tables are turned, and the preachers get a taste of their own medicine. Many of those who think of themselves as secular purists can't bring themselves to imagine for even a split second that a woman might actually *want* to wear the veil, out of religious piety or even as an aesthetic preference. It's peculiar that the ostentatiously worn beards and tunics of Muslim men should never have prompted such widespread exasperation. The claims of liberty, the explanations that these Muslim women offer—many of them single, and some of them university-educated—do not seem convincing. Even if they insist, they can't have entirely escaped the pressure of a father, a brother, a husband, or a religious leader. After all, they're only women, and they are not recognized to have a free will of their own. And there you have it, the subject at hand.

— Discredit of the movement can also come from certain activists fighting against other forms of discrimination. In their opinion, what we're dealing with here is a mutiny of spoiled children, white women, wealthy and famous, sufficiently privileged in any case to make their voices heard. Although the #MeToo hashtag was invented by a black woman, Tarana Burke, to share the stories of low-income girls and women of color, the movement only gained widespread media attention after the hashtag began to be shared by the very women who were best equipped to defend themselves. Movie stars, in some cases. Major revolutions often begin with the revolt of the most powerful among the powerless. Which is exactly what female movie stars are: powerful inasmuch as they are movie stars, but powerless inasmuch as they are women. In a ripple effect, the powerless among the powerless will then progressively begin to raise their voices as well. You cannot discredit a movement on the pretext that it seems only concerned with the privileged and the powerful. That said, you need to ask the right questions, you need to examine the foundations of society. The reason I wrote this book in the first place was in fact to show that #MeToo is not some passing fluke, some contingent phenomenon amidst the current array of forces at play. It's the beginning of one of the finest, most justified, incisive, and radical collective critiques of the Existential Situation of Women, which calls into question the most archaic and archetypal foundations of humanity.

Asking good questions, however, is not enough. A powerful social movement must also be popular and open. And that is certainly the case in this context. To an increasing degree, women in the less privileged classes of the population feel involved. They do not hesitate to express themselves on social media. As I write this, in the heart of the Ford Motor Company, a number of women have not only raised their voices against the sexual harassment to which they've been subjected, but also against the indifference with which their complaints have been met; no doubt because they're ordinary women, low-level employees, nameless factory workers. Their voices were ultimately heard in the pages of the *New York Times*.[2] Because of the unprecedented freedom of speech available in social networks on the Internet, #MeToo is well suited to make heard a steady accumulation of discrimination and inequality, what we call intersectionality. Women are speaking out about their experiences not only as women, but also as black women, as lesbian women, as unemployed women, as immigrant women. *Time* magazine named the women of the movement "the silence breakers," as well as the *Time* Person of the Year for 2017. On the cover were five women, clearly visible. The group included two major stars, actress Ashley Judd and singer-songwriter Taylor Swift, but also lobbyist Adama Iwu, software engineer Susan Fowler, and agricultural worker Isabel Pascual (pseudonym). Not to mention the elbow of a hospital worker whose face cannot be seen, representing the unnamed women who came forward anonymously.

Let me add that this movement cannot help but enrich, by cultural contagion, the critique of the array of discriminations concerning sexual choice (the right to freely experience the sexuality that one chooses) and gender freedom (the right to be recognized in the gender identity that best fits us). Because through #MeToo, and aside from the multiplicity of situations, the fundamental question raised is—let me say it again—that of a full and whole recognition of the free will of all human beings.

— A fourth way of sidestepping the issue is by calling for a solution that takes the form of a moral rearmament. We hear statements of the following tenor: "We must suppress shameless forms of behavior. We must fight against promiscuity. Sex, as a responsible act, has become devalued in our degenerate present-day societies. The sacred bonds of marriage are no longer respected. Nothing has worked right since the seventies, since the advent of the Pill and abortion." We can sense that this neo-puritan drift could easily result in new levels of segregation: men with men, women with women.

Especially in the Anglo-Saxon world, and especially in the United States, with the prevalence of separate cultures, boys' nights and girls' nights, the proliferation of prohibitions, the legalisms governing intimate behaviors. This tendency, of course, is even stronger in extremely religious societies, with lines of reasoning of this ilk: "It's because we want to protect women from harassment and rape that we cover the faces of *our* women and that we separate them from men." Even societies that are considered to be the most liberal aren't proof against projects of gendered apartheid. A major German railway company did not hesitate to introduce women-only carriages in February 2016. And women-only carriages have been available in Japan since 2010. To claim to protect women doesn't settle the problem, instead it simply subscribes to the reinforcement of discriminatory prejudices. Women aren't asking to be protected by men—they can guess full well at the kind of restrictions that would entail to their personal freedom—rather, they are asking to be respected unconditionally.

— Yet other writers declare their uneasiness about these "puritanical trends" that #MeToo is presumably representing. It's the fifth and last way of denigrating the movement: supposedly we're making no distinction between a serial rapist and a vulgar lothario who grabs a young woman's ass in the waning hours of a drunken evening out. Whether male or female, these scolds reproach the women who take a stand against harassment

for trying to prohibit innocent flirtation, the gentle art
of seduction which, in their view, ought necessarily to
be embellished with the improprieties that spice up life.
These occasionally unconscious misogynists, who see
themselves as good-hearted, fun-loving pranksters, are
every bit as mistaken as the puritanical, segregationist
social warriors. We shouldn't be confused about the
differences between an inappropriate act on the subway, a lewd remark at the entrance to a nightclub, daily
sexual harassment on the job, and an involuntary sex
act. These various acts should certainly be ranked in severity. That said, and leaving aside their relative degrees
of severity, they all bespeak a form of behavior that fits
perfectly into the larger structure of male domination
over women. It is this structure, aside from the infre-
quent cases of men accused and called out by name,
that is the chief target of the women leading the revolt
these days. If we start from the multiplicity of such concrete situations, we soon glimpse the actual dimensions
of the current condition of women. The eyewitness
accounts being set forth are in no way meant to limit
sexual freedom. If anything, they are actually calling for
its expansion: but in the spirit of fair reciprocity. And
that changes everything. We cannot have freedoms that
redound to the detriment of the freedoms of others. The
open letter published in the January 9, 2018, edition of
the newspaper *Le Monde*[3] and signed by one hundred
women, among them the actress Catherine Deneuve
and the novelist Catherine Millet, bespeaks a surprising

level of ignorance. I believe that the signatories to this letter, who declare their fear of a puritanical regression, simply never bothered to read what is actually written on the #MeToo feed. What's more, they seem to confuse those who persistently importune women with genuine flirtation. In the first case, those who importune fail to respect the consent of others; in the second case, one strives to win that consent; or to be exact, one takes pleasure in obtaining it. That is the essential charm of the true game of seduction.

The women who have spoken up on Twitter have no interest in emasculating males. They have no intention of prohibiting anything that is mutually desired. None whatsoever. They're not demanding exclusive train cars. They're not calling for the criminalization of any practices in and of themselves, as long as they are consensual. Let's not pretend we don't understand. The problem has nothing to do with fellatio, cunnilingus, or any erotic foreplay or byplay. It's not about pickup artists, about people eyeing each other up, surreptitiously fondling each other under the table, getting cheap thrills, engaging in the art of seduction, or even serenading someone. There's nothing bad about sex for these women in revolt. Their position stands in sharp contrast with the horror a prudish priest or monk might feel about the *impurity* of the female sex, or the excitement a sexist male pickup artist might feel at the thought of *defiling* his targets.

We have to recognize that sexual liberation—above and beyond the high-flown theoretical pronouncements of late-sixties revolutionaries and the widespread adoption of the Pill—has for decades now been more of a boon for men than for women. As long as human beings continue to be thought of as lambs, it is always going to be the wolf that profits most from greater freedom of action. It makes no sense to proclaim liberty without a corresponding concrete equality. But since the turn of the millennium, the situation has changed, as the number of women enjoying full financial independence and openly enjoying their sexual freedom has grown considerably. They don't reject out of hand the games of seduction—as those who so disingenuously blur the differences between flirtation and predation pretend to believe—they simply wish to get as much enjoyment out of it as the men. On the other hand, they refuse to go on playing the complaisant lambs, always willing to be manipulated, rejected, or devoured according to men's moods, appetites, and circumstances. They want to take active part, in concrete terms, wholeheartedly and on an equal basis, in all the forms of intimate and leisure pursuits—to say nothing of sexual enjoyment—that make up the content of a fulfilled and fulfilling human life. They definitely want to participate. They want to take part in life, out in the great world, whatever the time of day or night. Without having to cross to the other side of the street. Without having to lower their gaze or avert their eyes. They're calling for real-life equality, and it's a genuine cri de cœur. They want to be part of a concrete form of universalism. They want a transition from *potential modernity* to *actual modernity*.

THE TRANSCENDENTAL VALUE
OF CONSENT

Leaving aside the scenes described at #MeToo, which range from the grotesque to the abject, what is at stake is nothing less than the question of women's Being. The resemblance to the Valladolid debate concerning the ontological status of Native Americans is striking. In the middle of the sixteenth century, many European Catholics struggled to recognize that non-white "savages" actually possessed a soul, even though according to Catholic doctrine, which by definition addressed all of humanity (a humanity that, of course, European Catholics eagerly wished to evangelize), there could be no question about it. But to acknowledge that they possessed a soul, full and complete, would ipso facto prohibit those same Europeans from treating them as passive objects, coercible as one pleased. To deny that they possessed souls was tantamount to authorizing the colonists to own them and dispose of them as if they were, in fact, inanimate objects. The protagonists of this debate, in order to maintain a semblance of Christian consistency, pretended to be interested in quite other matters. There was much discussion, for example, of the cruelty of Native American rituals, the bloody sacrifices, which could certainly be shocking spectacles that cried out for prohibition, as a fine and indirect way of offering a debased image of them. But the real question at stake here was whether or not to attribute to them all the benefits and rights that go with a soul just like "ours."

In any great debate, there are prominent figures who are defending their interests or their principles. Or else, perhaps, their personal interests *disguised* as principles. Nowadays, on the one hand, we have women suffering from the reality that, in this, the early twenty-first century, the worth of their free will was denied and belittled. On the other hand, we have men (and women) who are seemingly well intentioned even as they still refuse to attribute a transcendental value, unquestionable a priori, to the consent of women; refusing, in other words, to acknowledge any real Free Will on their part, i.e., a full Subjectivity, which is tantamount, in the final analysis, to recognizing their full Humanity. In point of fact, after the advent of the Aufklärung—the philosophy of the Enlightenment—in the eighteenth century, it was no longer the possession of an individual soul that gave a person their humanity, rather, it was their *transcendental subjectivity.* That is to say, the recognition of an "inner sense," an autonomous ability to think, in humanity taken as a whole.[4] *Spontaneous* by nature (without material causes),[5] the Will that characterizes this pure Subject cannot be reduced to mere *receptivity* (the conditioning of the outside world). Politically, such a subject is, therefore, "the equal of any other."[6]

∂ψ

Beginning with this principle of the Free Subject, no one has ever offered a better definition than the philosopher Immanuel Kant of the larger program of modernity: the recognition in all human beings of the ability "to make use of one's own understanding without direction from another."[7] This is the original source of the meaning of modern democracy. The debate over the consent of women, begun by #MeToo, cast a stark spotlight on the fact that even now they have been left out of that admirable program. Officially, many insist that no one is denying women's Free Will, in keeping with the universalist principles that are now an integral element of the law, while still behaving as if a woman's free will were always somehow incomplete. As if a woman could never be capable of fully expressing her wishes. Instead, women simper, they flirt, they provoke, they seduce. When they seem to be saying no, it's not a genuine no, but rather in accordance with the perfect model of the Hollywood western, where it's only natural to see John Wayne slap and clutch in his brawny arms the woman who at first refuses to let herself be kissed. Because deep down, this is what the reluctant woman actually wants *without knowing that she wants it*: to be hunted down and trapped by the hero. The man knows better than she herself knows what it is she *really* wants. He can therefore legitimately substitute his own will for the will of the woman he desires, because her will is always slightly defective.

WHAT THE MYTH OF
PRINCE CHARMING TELLS US

A militant seducer imagines himself not like a monstrous Weinstein figure—a rapist, pure and simple—but like the prince who kisses Sleeping Beauty. A kiss stolen in this manner isn't really stolen at all. Likewise, a roaming hand that grazes butt cheeks in a packed subway car is never considered to be entirely out of order. Because a woman is always a little bit asleep, ready to be kissed, touched, awakened to a desire not yet known to her. If she raises her voice—even if it's to shout "Rape!"—it's only because she doesn't yet realize what it is she really wants. The fable of Sleeping Beauty cuts right to the core of the matter. It offers a depiction of the fragile, delicate, passive woman who falls into a deep sleep while awaiting her Prince Charming, without even knowing it. For a hundred years. Which is to say an eternity, minus an embrace. Just the same as Snow White or Cinderella, Sleeping Beauty has no intrinsic value, except for whatever value the man confers upon her, with royal graciousness. The prince's love is voluntary. The love of the penniless waif, or the slattern, or the delicate wench who pricks her finger with a spindle, in contrast, is pure receptivity. He loves her. She, in response, settles for falling in love, literally falling into his arms, arms that wrap around her and lift her into the air. He is active. He clutches her. She is fulfilled. He fulfills her. She is passive, swept away by passion, fully bestowed by him. The myth of Cinderella and the myth of Snow White are especially interesting on a social plane, suggesting that the future princess was nothing more than unexploited capital, until her meeting with the man who honored her with his choice. The prince therefore confers upon her an enviable status, endowed by his act, his kiss, his forceful grip, by carrying her in his arms before the admiring crowd. The woman is thus elevated to royal rank by the magic of a kiss and the strength of a pair of manly arms.

Sleeping Beauty takes it even further—especially in Giambattista Basile's original version, which dates back to the turn of the seventeenth century, and is titled *Sun, Moon, and Talia*. That version sprang in its turn from folktales dating back to the first half of the fourteenth century. There is none of the dramatic sentimentality that was later leavened into the mix, first by Charles Perrault, and then by the Brothers Grimm. It tells the tale of a king who ventures deep into the forest while hunting, there to discover a princess, all alone and fast asleep, in a solitary cottage in the middle of nowhere. This is Princess Talia. The king falls in love with her at first sight and, in no more time than it takes to tell the tale, rapes her as she sleeps. This sleeping beauty, completely passive (fast asleep), the object of the man's *legitimate* desire and of the urgent and necessary satisfaction of his desire, fails to awaken either during or after the act. She experiences neither pain nor pleasure. She becomes pregnant and gives birth nine months later, still in the same state of slumber. When she finally awakens—as a result of the sucking of one of her children who accidentally draws the soporific splinter from her flesh while attempting to suckle—she is cast into a state of ecstasy when she lays eyes on her offspring. Rape, thus, is a blessing. By means of rape, she has been enabled to awaken to her true life. First and foremost by becoming a mother. It never even crosses the princess's mind that there could have been an assault upon her person. It was the best of luck to be raped. For that matter, it wasn't really rape at all, because the very idea that Talia may have possessed free will simply isn't brought up. The mere thought that she might not have consented to the act of sex is simply devoid of meaning in the fable's logic. The moral of the story is striking: *Those whom fortune favors find good luck even in their sleep.*

WOMAN AS CAPITAL

The slogan *"Mon corps m'appartient"* ("My body belongs to me"), which was chanted in the 1970s by the members of the French MLF (Mouvement de libération des femmes, or Women's Liberation Movement), was not limited to the debate about abortion. The violent controversy that split France right up until the passage of the 1975 law legalizing the voluntary termination of pregnancy, pushed into the background the deeper, more anthropological meaning of that renowned feminist statement. In fact, for some 6,000 years, and in all societies, women's bodies have been traded, bartered, hoarded, and exploited by men as if they were fungible items of capital. In contrast with what might be suggested by the surrounding uproar, the #MeToo movement isn't indulging in vengeful outpourings, but instead underscores the persistence of the capitalistic status of the female body. It's a collective undertaking of a new awareness of reality, transcendence of self, and resilience. And it's also an acute and convergent appeal, which the slogan of the MLF sums up perfectly: no, women's bodies aren't capital that belongs to those who seize it. They belong to autonomous subjects endowed with Free Will.

The anthropologist Marshall Sahlins believes that one of the origins of capitalism—which he claims dates back to the Neolithic period and not, as Marx believed, to the advent of bourgeois society—was the idea of *capitalizing on women's bodies* by men. By collecting women dependent on his prestige, the "big-man," the man who is striving to impose himself as powerful, must multiply his own means of production.[8] This is in contrast to the hunter-gatherers of earlier Stone Age eras, who supposedly lived in a state of nonviolent abundance.

The vision set forth by Sahlins, who conducted research in the field on the islands of Fiji and Hawaii in a quest to find "primitive economies," seems, however, just a touch idyllic. It is reminiscent of that of Margaret Mead, whose research in the 1930s on another Pacific island, Samoa, supposedly found a state of virtually total sexual license among women—a thesis which has since been disproved. We know

now that women have been excluded from high-status activities since the most primitive times. In the Paleolithic age, they were often put in charge of gathering, an activity that provided the group with their essential nutrition for subsistence, but which was held in low esteem. The men went off to hunt, an activity that was highly respected but which was far less reliable, and a less significant means of sustenance. The economic contribution women provided was greater, and yet their social status was lower. Men, therefore, lived off the backs of women. This switcheroo, this genuine hijacking of wealth, lies at the roots of what Christine Delphy calls the "patriarchal political economy."[9]

Let's take advantage of this opportunity to explode once and for all a fiction that stubbornly refuses to die. Namely, the supposed existence of matriarchal societies, run by women or at least egalitarian in terms of gender. There are certain authors who have speculated that hunter-gatherer societies, of which thirty or so specimens still survive today, might be close to the state of nature as Jean-Jacques Rousseau imagined it. Now, even in the societies where women enjoyed the greatest privileges, such as among the Iroquois, men were still considered to be superior. The men devoted their time to hunting and waging war, while the women were restricted to less valued tasks.[10] Here, there is a basic confusion between a genuinely matriarchal society, which is mere fiction, and a matrilineal society, where ancestral descent is traced through the female line, as is the case in Judaism, among the Mbuti people, or in the Jivaro or Iroquois tribal communities. In reality, women do enjoy better conditions in these societies, but they are by no means egalitarian.[11] In a similar line of thinking, reference is made to the practice of polyandry—when one woman marries multiple men, which is common in certain societies—in support of the notion of the existence of islands of women's liberty. But whether you're talking about the Spartans, as cited by Xenophon, or the Aché of Paraguay, studied by the anthropologist Pierre Clastres, or perhaps certain Tibetan groups, you cannot help but notice that the women in these societies are all clearly dominated as well. The sole difference is that the men in these societies are allowed to *share* the possession of a single woman.

Without falling for an idealized vision of the Stone Age, it does seem, however, that if women were already assigned to low-prestige domestic tasks, it was beginning with the Neolithic revolution that the women themselves became a form of *domesticity*. Something that lay at men's disposal, a source of prestige and power. The accumulation of women only enhanced the prestige of men. The tribal chief—followed by the most "important" men—would keep the largest possible number of feminine "livestock" or "chattel." Hence the constant quest for surplus, for productivity, for accumulation of material wealth in order to be able to maintain their women and guard them against other men. That in turn led to agriculture, the breeding and keeping of animal livestock, slavery, and economic inequality, with its attendant frustration and endemic violence, which in turn led to the need to stem that violence by means of political institutions endowed with independent armed forces.

However caricatural it may seem, this correlation between the reduction of women to the state of *objects* to enhance men's prestige and the genesis of the patriarchal economy (in a more unjust and violent society) remains a very fertile instrument for understanding the present day. We can also see that the concept of the harem is not unique, as some may think, to Muslim, Middle Eastern, or Asian cultures. Nowadays, polygamy is practiced in sub-Saharan Africa more than anywhere else. In Chad, one of the three most polygamous countries on Earth—to a far greater extent than any Arab nation!—the number of polygamous Catholics is much higher than the number of polygamous Muslims.[12]

THE PRICE OF WOMEN

Measuring a man's status by the number of women he possesses—or to whom he's married, which amounted to the same thing until relatively recent times—was standard practice in nearly all cultures. An available labor force, female bodies were first and foremost a source of capital to be secured, shown off, exploited, and traded. In the eighteenth century in America, black girls and women destined to serve as sex slaves (*fancies*) for white men could be sold for five times the price brought by a black male slave destined to toil in the fields.

The owners of these female slaves could enjoy them sexually (take pleasure from their bodies), in terms of labor (as housekeepers), and symbolically (by showing them off in society). They served the functions of reproductive spouse (mother), trophy wife, mistress, prostitute, and housekeeping slave (*housekeeper* or *maid* are exquisitely feminine terms: even now, male housekeepers are a rarity), sex slave, nursemaid (nanny), and cook. They could combine several different functions (reproductive spouse, trophy wife, and nanny) in cases where the household was living in straitened circumstances, or be limited to a single function (either mistress or trophy wife or child-bearer) if the household was relatively well-off.

As one must do with any other substantial investment, it is necessary to tend to the maintenance of women. They are like so many jewels that must be cared for. Their hair must be highlighted and crimped, their bodies clad in expensive dresses, and their facial features accentuated with makeup or, nowadays, transformed through cosmetic surgery. In ancient Greece, women might be excluded not only from political life (deprived of the right to participate in the deliberation of decisions about the city's fate by speaking in the space of public debate, on the agora) and civil life (such as the right to own property), but also from the nobler aspects of love life. Their bodies, "excessively" dependent on the reproductive function, in contrast with the bodies of ephebes, for instance, were viewed as inappropriate for the finer feelings, felt or stirred, of unfettered sentiment that went hand in hand with genuine love. Even when a woman was not confined to the *oikia*, the domain of the kitchen and childbearing, and her beauty was praised, it was praised for her magnificent passivity. Infinitely precious, perhaps, but like an object you might simply possess, comparable to a painting. A piece of capital cannot enjoy the world in general and take sexual pleasure in particular; enjoyment in general and sexual pleasure in particular are taken *from* "it." If a woman is versed in the arts, that, once again, is for the enjoyment of men, much like a Japanese geisha.

The female serf in the Middle Ages, while she was not worthy of marrying to a feudal lord, still at the very least owed him her virginity before her future husband—of her same social standing—could enjoy her flesh. This *droit du seigneur* or *jus primae noctis* continued in implicit practice until the twentieth century in various new forms. The doctor, especially the chief physician, with the nurse. The airline pilot with the stewardess. The executive with his secretary. The politician with his campaign manager. The producer with the actress. The man offers his status. The woman offers her body. Like all forms of capital, a woman is assessable. Her beauty, her curves, her complexion, her refined education all contributed to her value. That which is rarest is also obviously most valuable. Hence the importance assigned to virginity.

Virginity ensures, in that spirit, a more complete possession. The female body is viewed as a fungible good, subject to depreciation through wear. If never previously penetrated, it is considered to be brand-new. Though virginity is no longer the social prerequisite it once was, the ghost of virginity hardly seems banished from the present world, given that thousands of young girls nowadays are currently on the Internet, offering to sell their first sex act, at prices that can reach sums of millions of dollars. For a woman to sleep with a man means she loses her virtue. If the tables are turned, male virtue remains intact. If anything, it's enhanced. Male virginity, for that matter, has no value. Men talk of *getting rid* of their virginity, whereas a woman *loses* her virginity. Frequenting a brothel might have formed part of the education of a young man—not so long ago. And people worry if a boy isn't interested in girls. Contrariwise, a girl who pays too much attention to boys is suspected of being immoral. In other words, she might lose value. Even today, it's not uncommon for a man to denigrate a woman who has had *too many* lovers before him— and even to experience what one could call *retrospective jealousy* within the couple. She depreciates in his eyes. He thinks she must no longer respect herself, that she is an *easy girl*. Such a reaction from a man scrutinizing his partner's sexual past to make sure of her value is a perfectly capitalistic idea. This "depreciation through use" is coupled with "natural depreciation": the woman's advancing age. Even now, it's not uncommon to see an elderly millionaire strolling about with a young lingerie model. The reverse is far less common, even if it has become more likely. And still, perfectly shaped bodies of young women are displayed on posters and in ads, as if in shop windows, as if they were available for purchase, to be taken home and consumed, depicting them once again as luxury articles.

GIRLS GET IN FREE

Why is there a "girls get in free" policy in certain nightclubs? Of course, this has nothing to do with any personal respect for the girls. It's simply because their presence ensures that the club will attract male customers. If men still think of women as gift packs to be fought over, women have internalized the game. Traditionally women have been educated to perceive their own bodies as objects to be enjoyed, and that enjoyment as something to be negotiated. American-style rules of dating are a version of that negotiation. Women know that they have a strong interest in making men wait, to keep from undercutting their value in the eyes of a potential partner, even if that means denying or delaying their own desires. It all operates as if her enjoyment meant nothing to her. She is socially supposed to give a bit more of herself at every appointment with a potential lover. Making love is tantamount to giving away her body. The woman only considers the pleasure that she might draw from it on a secondary basis. Which means she doesn't consider herself as a body *taking* pleasure, but first and foremost as a body from which pleasure is *taken*. Contrariwise, in most cases, all that the man considers is the race, the victory, and the trophy. The pleasure of being able to tell his friends the next day that he "made it" with this girl is more intense than the act itself. There, too, it's not so much the enjoyment of the woman's body that constitutes the primary pleasure, but rather the prestige of *having had her.* Even if reality is much more complex, less exaggerated than these descriptions of men and women's attitudes and states of mind, no woman can overlook the fact that most basic male references to her sexuality are negative: getting fucked, getting hosed, being had, or becoming someone's "bitch."

This capitalistic view of women's bodies can be even more clearly detected in modern literature: behind the romantic depiction of their so-called extraordinary power. Even if the beautiful Heide, the heroine of Julien Gracq's novel *The Castle of Argol*, wasn't as *nonexistent* as Sleeping Beauty, the growth of her love for Albert is described thus: "in surrender and angelic trust—like a wholly submissive slave—[she] offered him like a prayer the treasures of her body utterly dedicated to him."[13] According to the narrator—and the narrator is always right—because she loved him, she was "wholly offered up to the one from whom, with every instant, she drew the miracle of the prolongation of her life."[14] And what about him, Albert, the lover, what does he want from her? Nothing other than "the possession of this splendid and surrendered body."[15] She lies "behind her inviolate beauty"; she makes him a "gift of herself"; she is "utterly abandoned to his mercy." There is not the slightest hint of any desire on her part, much less any discussion of her consent.

VIRILITY IS TRANSMITTED THROUGH WOMEN

As long as women continue to be treated as pieces of movable property, there will be no law capable of conferring rights upon them that are genuinely equal to the rights of men. The underlying principle of civil law will still be tacitly applied: "In the case of movable property, possession is tantamount to legal title." Just to be clear: the woman—who can be moved and traded away—belongs to the man who possesses her. The prince chooses, kisses, and sweeps the princess off her feet, who therefore, ipso facto, becomes his. She gives him her body, and he, in return, confers upon her a certain social standing. Obstacles can arise. But beginning from the very moment he takes possession of her and sweeps her off her feet, the transaction is understood. Even if it should entail some conflict; she has no say in the matter.

The case of the beautiful Helen of Troy is an eloquent example. Helen's essential quality was that of being the loveliest woman on earth; and for that matter, she herself was the product of a visit paid by Zeus himself to the bed of Helen's mother Leda, wife of Tyndareus (who was himself no less than the king of Sparta). That divine rape engendered feminine perfection. Helen, this absolute beauty who was so widely yearned after, was married off to the Greek king Menelaus, the first to win her, but she was then abducted, and from that day forth, reappropriated, by the Trojan prince Paris. Helen's wishes, the very idea that she might have a preference, counted for nothing. All of Greece—the Greece of men, to be sure, the land of heroes—led by Agamemnon, went to war against Troy to *take back* Helen. Dragged around from one owner to another, she was the most magnificent piece of property that a man or a nation could hope to possess. The story of the founding of Rome also revolves around a story of rape and abduction. Romulus and his brothers-in-arms needed to *get* women to populate their future city, so they stole the women of a neighboring people, the Sabines. The mass abduction of the Sabine women is sung as an act of great valor at the very birth of Rome. In both cases, that of the Trojan war and that of the founding of Rome, the seizing of women buttressed the virility of the nation as a whole.

Women, then, belong ipso facto to the conquering tribe; sometimes as brides, most frequently in the role of slaves. Nowadays, women can still be considered plunder of war. Rape itself may become a weapon. Over the course of the series of consecutive civil wars that bloodied certain portions of Liberia between 1989 and 2003, 90 percent of the women living in the regions involved had been raped. You humiliate your enemies by raping—by possessing, by owning—their women. Rape is a still-current fashion of consummating one's victory. Of savoring one's triumph. Of proving to oneself one's "natural" superiority.

A romantic abduction and a warlike rape both share the same structure. The ravisher deprives his victim of all independent free will. At the same time, *he*, the "hero," in contrast, is virilized, becoming more manly. *She*, in contrast, has no options but to submit in pain and sorrow or else to fall head over heels in love. In either case, she is subjugated. Even if, in the latter case, she sinks into the delights of being *ravished* by her *ravisher*. Once he's taken possession, the new owner or master is obliged to defend his property from the other males. Ulysses, by leaving his faithful spouse Penelope in Ithaca, exposed her and himself to the covetousness of the suitors. A woman cannot be left unguarded without her master. If her husband is traveling and one may reasonably expect him never to return, like Ulysses on his interminable odyssey, then the wife is once again put on the market. Her will counts for nothing. Only wily stratagems allowed Penelope to put off her suitors, delaying them for twenty long years until Ulysses returned. She is a woman who waits. She has no option but to give evasive answers, to shy away. Procrastinate. For that matter, she hadn't even had a say in the choice of her current husband, the man to whom she was remaining so stubbornly faithful. She had in fact been given to him as a trophy, offered as the first prize at the athletic competitions held at her own father's behest, a prize of which Ulysses was the fortunate winner.

Both sports and war are inherently virilizing pursuits. Men face off in these activities in order to captivate or simply capture women. The women, of course, are therefore excluded from either activity. Let us remember that *vira* in Sanskrit means both man (male) and hero (victorious warrior). Athletic competition is a simulacrum of war in peacetime. Even today, sports teams wear the colors of their nation, their region, city, or group.

Because athletics is *the* virilizing, manly activity by definition, both for the individual and the collective, girls still today have great difficulties in getting ahead in the field. The French women's soccer team, OM, the Olympique de Marseille, has been for many years much more successful than its male counterpart. And yet, no one seems to be aware of these outstanding athletes. The soccer matches that OM competes in so brilliantly and with such brio are attended by almost no one. Not even women soccer fans. The same goes with baseball, football, handball, and so forth, even if things are slowly changing. Obviously, we still think a woman's proper place is in the home, not on the battlefield or at the stadium. When it comes to sports, women can be sexy cheerleaders, there to whip up enthusiasm among the male spectators. At the very most, they can distinguish themselves in contests that allow them to express their *natural* qualities of charm, grace, and finesse, such as artistic ice skating or acrobatic dance.

The fact that the 2019 Women's World Cup was able to generate for the first time a real global enthusiasm, comparable to its male counterpart, demonstrates a genuine cultural shift, because it directly concerns our social imaginary. These international players are finally being seen as true "warriors," just as impressive as the men.

One of the most glaring forms of discrimination is the outright refusal to establish mixed-gender teams in most collective sports, such as soccer or handball. As if a woman could only be a handicap to a team. Or the refusal to allow men and women to compete individually against each other, in, say, tennis—if they wish. And since mental weakness is deduced as a corollary of physical weakness, the segregationist regime applies to competitive chess—again, supposedly, in order to protect the weaker sex. What then are we to say of the case of the young American female golfer Emily Nash, who at age sixteen came in first in a regional tournament, but was not allowed to be declared the winner? Regulations didn't account for the possibility of a girl winning; and so the boy who'd come in second on points was awarded the trophy. This event, which happened in November 2017, is emblematic of men's utter lack of preparation when it comes time to open the doors to their best-defended citadels.

WOMAN, INCOMPLETE IN BODY AND SOUL

So is it the *anatomical destiny of women*, to borrow Simone de Beauvoir's expression,[16] that forces them to remain on the sidelines? The appearance of the female body, less musclebound, smaller, less imposing than its male equivalent, constitutes the declared foundation of their inferiority. We must not labor under the illusion that we have rid ourselves of that imagery.

The argument that a woman's body is *naturally* more fragile deserves to be given attention only inasmuch as it is still so often brought to bear, if only to justify women's exclusion from certain professions that demand greater strength (and only, let it be clear, for *their* good and for the general good of society at large). As if their supposed physical weakness rightly relegated them to the background, or to some secondary status. Even de Beauvoir seems to give credence to at least a part of this thesis. Although de Beauvoir believes that women can—must!—rise up, and that they must certainly confront the power of men, she also feels that they must overcome their more *difficult* anatomical condition. The feminine body supposedly sacrifices its own proper functioning in the interest of the expected child. Menstrual cycles, for instance, constitute a challenge, a source of fatigue, and at times of extreme bouts of pain that are useless to the organism. The male organism, in contrast, operates on its own behalf, and would therefore seem to be more efficient. The argument itself is frail and fragile: some authors, in opposition to it, bring to bear the observation that the regular loss of blood actually regenerates the organism, which could partly explain women's greater longevity. Obviously, in the existentialist spirit, women are encouraged to liberate themselves from that biological situation, and write the terms of their own destiny. In order to ensure that their own liberty *exists*: "One is not born, but rather becomes, a woman."[17]

The other argument that is often brought up directly concerns heterosexual intercourse, which could not take place, it is pointed out, without an erect penis, a clear expression of male desire. On the other hand, a woman's body is always, so to speak, open to sexual intercourse, whether she wants it or not, to such an extent that a sleeping woman, such as Sleeping Beauty, or even a dead woman could be the victim of a man's sexual assault, whereas the reverse would be impossible. This vision of physiological inferiority and of the instinctive primacy of men's desire devalues feminine desire; which would naturally therefore be contingent in nature, a mere response to masculine desire. In the final analysis, that means considering female consent as somehow also being contingent by its very nature.

ℎℒ

From the degrading description of women's bodies and sex organs, we can deduce degrading moral judgments. Aristotle wrote that "a male is male in virtue of a particular ability, and a female is female in virtue of a particular inability."[18] During the sex act that makes reproduction possible, the woman provides nothing but the material of the human being that will come into the world, whereas the man injects a soul into that human being. The woman's morphological shortcoming, her physical incompleteness, correlates with moral incapacity, her lack of a soul, which justifies her resulting juridical and political incapacity. This entanglement between an incomplete body and the lack of soul is found as well in Plato, who writes that "only males are created directly by the gods and given souls."[19] As a punishment for their cowardice and their weakness, certain men may be reincarnated as women. Contrariwise, a woman's greatest hope would be to reincarnate as a man.

Traditional Buddhism more or less upholds the same position: it would be impossible to attain Awakening with a woman's body. Here, too, we move confusedly from the stigmatization of the "weakness" of the feminine body, woman's "incomplete" sex organ, to her less stern personality, her poor intelligence, her absence of a soul, and her lack of willpower, all of which result in her inferior position in society.

Sigmund Freud reinforced the view of a negative feminine psyche bound up with a woman's body: a woman sees herself as having been deprived of a phallus, the notorious *penis envy* of the young girl. The equivalent in young boys is the castration complex. The girl feels bad because she hasn't got a penis and the boy because he could lose it. The only positive organ is the male one. The libido is thus a fundamentally masculine force . . . even within women, as if feminine desire wasn't autonomous, and didn't possess a positive aspect of its own. Freud thus fits into the structural continuity of overarching symbolic oppositions: a woman is lunar while a man is solar; water is feminine while fire is masculine; humidity is feminine whereas dryness is masculine; strength is masculine while suppleness is feminine; a woman is all shadows and dim light, while the man is bright light and sunshine. She is the earth-mother and the fertile, abyssal sea, he is the clear, blue sky. The symbols can change from one culture to another. But consistently the man is the active element, while the woman is the passive one. After all, don't we say that a woman is either frigid (saying she "really needs a good fuck") or hot (calling her an "easy lay" or a "slut")? We describe a woman as a malleable material, without a soul, that doesn't exist except in terms of what is done or not done to "it."

RAPE CULTURE

This symbolic opposition or contrast, confusedly based on the *natural* physical difference, still looms large in terms of the role it plays in excusing sexual predators and justifying sexual harassers. Supposedly the man is active by his very nature. He has to sow his wild oats. He needs to target and touch the women that he desires. Whereas the woman, who is supposedly passive by nature, must wait until John Wayne or some other cowboy sets his sights on her. Sexual harassers, therefore, are simply doing their job as men. We can certainly see groups of tipsy (or perfectly sober) young men out on Saturday night egging each other on to put their virility to the test in the game of sexual hunting and gathering. This allows them to prove that they are real men. The shyest of them all will be mocked and ridiculed: he is clearly too *effeminate*, maybe even a homosexual! In the same spirit, they might shout out to some young woman as they pass her on the street, even though she hasn't paid them the slightest notice (though of course they think she is secretly hoping for nothing more): "You got a nice tight ass on you." If by any chance she were to react badly to that kind compliment, in defiance of this utterly natural expression of their *male-itude*, then of course they would denounce her as a slut, a whore, or a cunt. More insults reducing the young woman to little more than her sex organ might be showered upon her, with the greatest possible slathering of obscenity.

This kind of behavior is by no means uncommon. Indeed, it is structural. It dates back to time immemorial and is still handed down in schoolyards. Starting in high school, a young woman with a reputation for having had numerous lovers might well still be treated as a "slut," whereas, in the same case, a young man will more likely be treated as a "lady-killer" (the word speaks for itself) or "player." My fifteen-year-old daughter recently came into our house in tears, having been sent home by the assistant principal of the high school—of the *public* high school, let me make that point clear—on account of her supposedly inappropriate attire. She had allegedly tried to attract the eyes of her male classmates by wearing an excessively short skirt. The assistant principal's closing words had been scathing: "If anything happens to you, I wouldn't be a bit surprised." If we take it from the assistant principal, it's up to girls to restrain themselves. Otherwise, they're offering proof of *ill will*, a negative intent, an *absence of will* equivalent to a perverse, secret, shadowy, perhaps subconscious intent: they are "asking for it." A girl should always expect to be pursued by predators who are, by so doing, merely innocently following their inborn virile nature. "Boys will be boys," as the American expression enshrined in popular culture would have it. The girl, on the other hand, is guilty of raising her eyes, smiling, swiveling her hips, wearing a plunging neckline, being too shameless or provocative, thereby confirming her status as potential prey. It would never occur to anybody to tell a boy or young man to avoid drinking and going out at night lest he run the risk of raping any young women he happens to run into.

෴

The transmission of this "differential valence of the sexes," to borrow Françoise Héritier's expression, dates back to the earliest dawn of humanity. In traditional societies, the initiation ritual validates the transition from adolescence to adulthood. These initiation rituals often entailed physical and psychic tests and ordeals from which the young man had to emerge victorious in order to be able to take his rightful place among men. The difficulty of these challenges might be merely symbolic. But in any case, it was a matter of allowing the male to prove his virility and his courage, to free himself, to outdo himself, to transcend his childish condition, and to affirm his independent will. In Rome, that was the moment when the son of a patrician could finally don the virile toga. For young girls, the tests were not an opportunity for them to outdo themselves, but rather for them to learn to submit, to follow, to comply with the wishes of men. A male might suffer degradation and humiliation, but it was up to him to resist and overcome them. This was how he would enjoy his body in its full capacity and, thereby, enjoy his place in society.

⊘

One might say, to the contrary, that the essence of female initiation is excision: privation of the enjoyment of one's own body. And, consequently, privation of the enjoyment of the world independently of men. Even without any physical excision, strictly speaking, female initiation is equivalent to a symbolic excision. Male initiation is a ritual of expansion and emancipation, while the initiation of a woman is a ritual of reduction and subjection, which can extend to include gang rape; in order to make it clear to her, in the depths of her flesh, that she is no longer in charge of her own sexuality. In India, still today, in certain Shaivist sects, the Brahmin (priest) is summoned to perform a ritual rape of the young bride-to-be before her wedding. As a matter of fact, in most cultures, the traditional wedding is in some sense an institutionalized rape. The bride-to-be must be a virgin. She must save herself for her future owner. The deflowering will be her initiation, administered by her husband, who thus becomes her master.

What is happening here is that sex is being used to *put the woman in her place*, beneath the male: to *put her down*, or *sub-jugate* her. So that she can realize in her very flesh her own incompleteness, and in order to ensure that she can define herself in no way other than as belonging to the male, and specifically to her husband. By the same token, just as the man presents himself to her as a demigod, she must perceive herself as a demi-man. Half a man. An eternally incomplete human being.

The submission of women is inscribed in the very symbolism of civilizations, in the details of their grammar. As we well know, in many languages, even if not so much in English as, for example, in French, the masculine gender wins out over the feminine, and even, we might well say, simply *sweeps the feminine aside.* The debate over inclusive writing is therefore by no means a frivolous undertaking. What's profoundly at stake here is the general abolition of this norm of submission. Weinsteinian sexual harassment—which is meant to *put women down,* the literal etymology of submission (*sub-mit,* "to put down"), which fantasizes about its own power while denying the existence of the desire, decision-making, and enjoyment of the other—is, in its purest state, a holdover from archaic female initiation rites.

THE IMPOTENCE OF VIRILITY

The original practice of systematic rape was meant to devalue women physically and morally to a sufficient extent that they could be seen as incomplete beings, thereby justifying their exclusion from social power. But why such dogged persecution? Because, in the final analysis, if men actually had originally been so certain of their superiority, physical first and foremost, they would never have bothered with such contrived actions. The reason is that men are not only *not* certain of their superiority, they are in fact deeply ridden with complexes about women and, as Françoise Héritier informs us, intimidated by the feminine reproductive power. Men are, in other words, making women pay for the exorbitant privilege of that natural advantage. Overlaid upon this complex would be the anguish of seeing women shed blood on a regular basis: a symbol of both life and death. And we should clearly recognize that there would be no reason, without such an obsession with impotence, for any such universal persecution; no other explanation for this drive to diminish women on the one hand and, on the other, to lord it over them, aggrandizing ourselves in comparison to and in front of them. This is the essential dynamic of virility.

It has been defended in several studies of paleoanthropology that even the weaker morphology of women could also be the product of this very same culture of domination.[20] According to this serious research, for almost 750,000 years, during the pre-Neanderthal era, long before human morphology had even stabilized, women were systematically deprived of meat, which was replaced in their diet largely by starches. Men were probably attempting to reserve for themselves the symbolic strength of animal flesh. The narrowness of women's shoulders, chests, and waists, their more fragile bone structure and musculature, therefore in part could date far back in time to that period of extended protein privation.

According to this theory, the current physical situation of women is in part the product of an older cultural construction, on top of very real genetic differences. This constant and universal "evolutionary pressure," even if it no longer involves the same food constraints, has relaxed only slightly as of the present day. The original goal of privation has been progressively, and quite perversely, replaced with the goal of shaping women's bodies into something desirable. That is the charm of fragility. We clamped waists, chests, and bosoms in corsets. This narrowed the figure to an hourglass shape and hampered women's breathing until it became a panting, delicate whisper. Men wore high heels at the court of Louis XIV—indeed, they were worn first and foremost by the king himself—to give them extra height. Worn by women, however, the heel grew narrower and narrower until it turned into the stiletto heel, which makes a woman's gait more perilous, challenging, gliding and dancelike and, ultimately, charming. The traditional Japanese men's *hakama*, an extremely loose and ample kimono bottom, is designed to accommodate an outgoing, vigorous gait in which, working from the *hara*, or center of gravity, the man fiercely throws his leg forward at each step. In contrast, the women's kimono clamps together hips, thighs, and calves as much as possible, all the way down to the ankles, like some silken sarcophagus. This forced Japanese women to walk with tiny, delicate steps. The slightest unforeseen obstacle might result in a fall. Even more cruel is the Chinese tradition that forced young girls to permanently imprison their feet in bandages to keep them from growing. Aside from the atrocious pain suffered throughout childhood and adolescence as a result of this foot-binding, the expected results when the girl reached adulthood were severely atrophied feet—yes, but so sweet and small!—and a perpetually painful gait—but so refined! The aesthetic canons of classical ballet, very much in keeping with the contemporary world of fashion, perpetuate this model of torture, by enshrining an ideal of feminine beauty predicated on the idea of an anorexic woman-child. So fine, so small, so skinny, so light, eyes glazed, sickly, as if pining away and ultimately vanishing. Wonderful in her fragility and passivity. Yet conversely, when the image exhibited is the even more pornographic and generous one of the courtesan with ample curves, then she too seems to become a prisoner of her shape, ready to be offered up on a silver platter and sampled hungrily by an eager male.

These physical obstacles have been culturally transmuted into qualities. Well, for the men, anyway, who can confidently measure their stature, their greatness, and their confident gait in contrast with this frail creature. And for the women, too, who wish to make themselves desirable in the eyes of the men, as well as in their own eyes. But there's more to it than that. These corporeal qualities are reflected in moral virtues. This leads to the construction of the feminine Eternal made up of modesty, delicacy, fidelity, virginity, purity, carefreeness, gentleness, altruism, self-abnegation, loving and maternal generosity, modesty, self-restraint, self-effacement, and timidity. In other words, submission is elevated to the status of Virtue, a pledge of the honor that any woman must jealously preserve intact. Feminine Virtue is the polar opposite of Virility.

Traditionally, Virtue was taught to women from their infancy until it was incorporated into their every gesture. A girl would learn timidity and modesty, just as boys learned fierceness and haughtiness. A girl who frees herself momentarily from the pillory of her fragility, because she dares to make a remark, or because she dares in *any* way, shape, or form, might well find herself considered foolish, gossipy, shallow, tomboyish, out of place, uncouth, and indecent. Everything points to a successful transmission of those values when the young woman defends her own submission by jealously preserving her virginity until marriage, when she can be more wholly possessed by her husband and dispossessed of her own self.

This patriarchal distinction between the force of masculine Virility and the modesty of feminine Virtue hasn't entirely disappeared. It still largely structures our individual libido and our collective mental representations. We can certainly rebel against it, whether we are men or women. Or else we can dig in and stubbornly protect those venerable old values. Voices have actually been raised—women's voices among them—in defense of Harvey Weinstein's roundly "violated" virility. The patriarchal civilization is in a state of crisis, indeed, perhaps in its death throes, with all the disquiet and uneasy that derives from that fact. In this precarious setting, the image of the manly man, protective in accordance with tradition, may be reassuring to some. The image of femininity, submissive, but protected, may still prove comfortable for many women in the face of uncertainty and the loss of reliable landmarks and lodestars.

THE ANGUISH OF FEMALE OVERKILL

By a stunning sleight-of-hand, this diminution proclaimed as a form of virtue would eventually become the very essence of womanhood. Women, supposedly, were born that way and it would be monstrous to think they could ever change. It would fly in the face of God's will and the laws of Nature herself: a blasphemy or a form of degeneracy. If a woman has to define herself in terms of a man and therefore shrink, self-effacing, into his shadow, it's because she's only half as human. It's what the great foundational myths tell us, beginning with the Bible story in which Eve is fashioned from one of Adam's ribs. In vain might we venture to establish a hierarchy among the religions. They all tell of woman's original infirmity. Most Greek philosophers and storytellers echo that description. Doubtless, this is one of the most far-reaching, vast, and farcical masquerades in human history. The problem is not religion, but the patriarchal culture. According to it, the female sex organ itself is nothing more or less than a truncated male sex organ, imperfect or even inverted according to certain cultures. It was not until the twentieth century that we finally bypassed this *phallomorphism* and finally recognized the physiological autonomy of women's sex organs.[21]

Nothing more clearly shows that this alleged feminine frailty, transmuted into grace, serves to conjure up the archaic sentiment of masculine impotence than the rage, condemnation, and repression that comes hurtling furiously down upon all those women who refuse to conform to it. One can sense on all sides the male fear of losing control. All of humanity's religions follow the same general scheme, with variations, of course. In the Bible, Eve is certainly the weaker member of the couple, born of Adam's flesh. Nonetheless, she is the temptress, the seductress, who brings about the catastrophe. She is "the door to the devil," wrote Tertullian. We must not trust her, we must put restraints upon her. Let us shift for a moment to different cultures: Buddhist monastic regulations impose far fewer restrictions on men than on women, with harsher punishments for the latter. Contemporary female tourists visiting Myanmar may still be surprised to discover that, unlike men, they are prohibited from applying gold leaf to the five Buddhas within the walls of the famous Hpaung Daw U pagoda on the shore of Inle Lake. According to the Koran, women must always be scrupulously supervised. Women are always suspected of transgressions. The slightest infraction, the mere fact of speaking to another man, may be taken by her husband as evidence of infidelity. We see the same general idea in the Christian New Testament, especially in the Epistle to the Corinthians, where Saint Paul condemns women to silence, for fear that a single subversive word might issue from their mouths. He leaves them but two paths to salvation, either motherhood or sainthood. The Virgin Mary is certainly sublime and revered, but merely as a passive receptacle of the divine. By Roman law, only female infidelity was punished, and punished quite severely, because the ancient Romans believed that woman is "the seat of a mysterious and supernatural power."[22] Until 1975, in the French Civil Code and Penal Code, it was easier to prove a woman had committed adultery, and far more harshly punished. And so on and so forth. From the earliest times, men have always had a panicky fear of women's freedom. The mythology of the Selk'nam people offers a fascinating illustration of this fact. Among this tribe of Tierra del Fuego, the women were subjected to a relentless and extremely brutal oppression, which was supposedly justified by the fact that in the beginning, it had been women, ultrapowerful and terrifying, who tortured men and held them in slavery.[23]

✍

Let us go back to the story of Genesis. Eve, incomplete, is rivaled by another mythical woman, Lilith, who was supposedly the true and whole original woman. She claimed to be equal to man and was therefore damned for all eternity. Lilith, hurled into the flames of hell, is the foremother of all the witches of the Middle Ages, the hysterics of the nineteenth century, and the sluts of the modern day. In the Middle Ages, a woman beyond a certain age who had neither married (thus not controlled by a husband) nor taken holy orders (thus not controlled by priests) was automatically suspected of either being a witch or possessed by the forces of evil. The case of the witchcraft trials held in seventeenth-century Loudun, France (dramatized in the 1971 Ken Russell film *The Devils*), is typical of the mass panic triggered by the freedom—especially the sexual freedom—of women who were accused of being possessed by the devil.[24] The solutions suggested by men: exorcism, lynching, or burning at the stake. In the final analysis, a witch is nothing other than a woman who is more independent than others, and to whom unlimited, invisible powers are immediately attributed, beyond the reach of men. These powers are typically connected to sexual energy, which is what witchcraft is really about.

This maddening fantasy of the overwhelming power of a free woman is the reverse of the masculine feeling of impotence. That the very word *impotence* directly designates the inability to have an erection in the presence of a woman, and that this could be such an immense problem, offers a strong confirmation that virility isn't such an all-powerful and uncontainable force, after all. Virility is the violent and overcautious reaction to men's feeling of impotence, which certainly comes first. Men have reduced women physically and symbolically in order to be able to exclude them from social competition. They strove to prevent equality for fear of having to measure themselves against, and be shown up by, the *potency* of the opposite sex.

THE WOMAN WHO CAN HAVE
ENDLESS ORGASMS

In the nineteenth century, the hysteric took the place of the witch. Bourgeois medicine took charge of the job of social control. Michel Foucault wrote about "the hysterization of women's bodies": bodies saturated with sexuality, perpetually on the brink of the abyss. Let's remember that the Greek word *hystera* means "uterus"! The father and the husband become middlemen for the doctor. Their family authority is thus in a certain sense backed up and given a scientific justification. The virginity and the absolute fidelity that are imposed on women are no longer theological requirements, but medical ones. "Scientific" doctrine, however, seems strangely modeled on the same blueprint as religious prejudices: there are no hysterical nuns, since by an overwhelming majority, it is prostitutes that the malady affects. The diagnosis is a way of warning women to stick to the straight and narrow.

By controlling his wife, a husband is simply protecting her good health. Since *he* has a naturally sound and healthy sexuality, inasmuch as it seems to him intrinsically limited, it is therefore up to him to place limits on *her* sexuality. This leads to a fascinating reversal: the sexual limits traditionally imposed upon women are now transformed into sanitary, medical considerations. *Apeiron*, the term for "boundless" or "unlimited," already designated chaos among the ancient Greeks. A "hysterized" woman would thus be a sort of abyss: a bottomless pit (the cause of chaos) which the male phallus (the cause of order) can never hope to fill. How can we help but see, looming in the shadows, unconfessed, the sheer anguish of men, who feel constrained by the number and quality of their erections? A man cannot come, cannot ejaculate more than a certain limited number of times, while, as they saw it, a woman can have endless orgasms, *to the brink of madness*. Her desire might never reach an end. The male's ultimate nightmare is of being engulfed by female desire.

Hence the preventive excision performed on women's consciences, and sometimes even on their bodies. A bourgeois husband still demands his fiancée's virginity and his wife's faithfulness, while he is held blameless for having a series of mistresses himself, as well as assiduously frequenting brothels. He wants to be able to hunt freely outside of the bedroom and remain the unquestioned master inside of it. With the excuse of protecting his wife from her own disordered natural state and the more general disorder of the outside world, he holds her captive. A jealous custodian of her virtue, in reality what he fears is the competition of her freedom, because he feels certain he'd be incapable of fulfilling her free desire on his own.

Molière had perfectly depicted this prison-like ideal in his play, *The School for Wives*: girls are taught ignorance in order to ensure they're inoffensive and innocent. An educated woman would simply be a monster. Those women who had that ambition were forced to conceal their true appearance behind the figure of a "great" man, such as the case of the Marquise du Châtelet, a brilliant female eighteenth-century mathematician who lived modestly in the shadow of Voltaire. In accordance with the traditional model, she was his mistress and remained faithful to him emotionally, sexually, and intellectually. Unlike *him*. She could easily have become the French Isaac Newton if only she hadn't been born a woman.

Certain of these women actually took on a masculine identity, at the risk of shocking society at large; one such was the
great nineteenth-century writer Aurore Dupin, who scandalized her respectable contemporaries by frequently dressing
in male attire, taking countless lovers, and using a masculine
pen name: George Sand. Even as a child, she rebelled against
the charm of *her* all-too-feminine fragility: "I felt just a bit
humiliated that he thought me such a little girl, and I soon
showed him I was a very resolute boy."[25] During a lecture she
delivered to an audience of surprised young female university students at Cambridge in 1928,[26] the English writer Virginia Woolf, who fought throughout her life to maintain her
independence, pointed out that, had William Shakespeare
been a woman, she would never have had even the slightest
chance of becoming the great playwright we now know and
love, because she would never even have been sent to school,
no matter how talented she might have proven to be from her
childhood on.

THE CULTURE OF IMPOTENCE

Under the guise of pseudo-medical discourse that speaks of
women, men are actually talking about themselves. More
precisely, even now, what they're talking about is their feeling of impotence. This is where male fantasies about penis
size come from, as well as male obsessions with the size of all
manner of things: cars, houses, watches. Calling a woman

a slut, with a direct reference to her sexual freedom, clearly bespeaks the same defensive reflex. Women are caught on the horns of a dilemma. They can either be denounced as witches, hysterics, or sluts, as a punishment for having dared to own themselves too openly. Or else they can be flattered, seen as wonderful, delightful, and abounding in charm, because they gracefully accept being dispossessed of themselves.

The twentieth century also saw its fair share of pseudoscience steeped in misogyny. The father of sociobiology, E. O. Wilson, who mixed Darwinism with Freudianism, seemed to enshrine the evolutionary superiority of man over woman. His theory, which dates back to 1975, provided antifeminists with an arsenal of weapons in the explosive years of sexual liberation. In Wilson's view, life is a struggle in which the male gained the upper hand because he has the most stamina, strength, and determination. In a word, because he is superior. The female is supposedly *naturally* inferior to the male. Wilson elided the collaborative relationship between the sexes, however essential it is to the survival and amelioration of the species, and overlooked the weight of evolutionary pressure on female morphology. Men, he alleged, have a tendency toward promiscuity because they have a vocation to spread their semen, which they produce to the point of overabundance. Women, who produce no more than one egg a month, and for a shorter period of their lives, supposedly need to economize the use of their body. They are forced to live in a cautious state of waiting, being both as attractive (presenting themselves in the light of their best features) and selective (avoiding "reckless" sexual relations) as possible. We really can't blame men, therefore, for their insistent and persistent courtships, in any and all occasions. Sexual harassment, in other words, redounds to the benefit of the species—as does feminine restraint. The methodology of sociobiology was called into question starting in the late 1980, and most of its theses have since been discredited.[27] But popular prejudices are remarkably stubborn and tenacious.

The words *witch, hysterical,* and *slut* are used to designate women who are "intolerable" because they behave independently. The use of these words, then, is meant to depict women's freedom as a form of deprivation. Since a witch does not belong to any particular individual man, she is supposedly possessed by the devil, while the hysteric instead is possessed by her malady, and the slut is possessed by all those men who take advantage of her debauchery. Men obstinately refuse to realize that a woman might simply wish to *enjoy* the world, independent of his supervision—in other words, that she might wish to be her own person. Forced to acknowledge the existence of women's orgasms after the Sexual Revolution of the 1960s, men quickly scrambled to turn them into a new indicator of their power. The feminine orgasm became a product of a manly performance. Men reinvented themselves as the absolute masters of feminine pleasure. Executioner of bodies and hearts, it was the man who wielded the weapon.

Men used sexual liberation to attempt to construct a new dominance. Feminine desire and pleasure remained dependent in nature; the man became the hero of the sex act, transporting the woman by loving her. It is he who desires and bestows the woman's pleasure, which becomes a gauge of his virility and, therefore, the object of his fear of failure. This fear would prompt millions of modern women to respond by faking those orgasms; a piece of trickery unveiled with wicked humor and brio by Meg Ryan in the 1989 film *When Harry Met Sally*, when Sally surprises Harry by faking an orgasm in front of him in a restaurant.

And so it is not women who define themselves in relation to men. Rather, it has been the opposite since the very beginning. The anxiety resulting from penis envy (*Penisneid*) isn't a female problem, as in the Freudian view, but entirely male. The phallic cult tries to steer women away from their own sexuality, from their own pleasure, and hence from their own independent enjoyment of life and their own positive identity. This is to ensure that they forget themselves, once and for all, for the benefit of men. Friedrich Nietzsche very rightly teaches that violence arises from a sense of helplessness. From a fear of being unequal to the task. Of being outdone by the *other*. As a result, one ensures that this *other* is kept out of competition in advance, lest one is forced to measure oneself against that other. This is the mechanism of racism. This is profound machismo. This is the deep-rooted meaning of the Weinsteinian desire to enjoy another's submission, to take pleasure from the very fact that she has been brought to her knees.

ESCAPING FROM THE GILDED CAGE

In order to be rid of male domination, it is not enough to stop the most blatant acts of violence. It is necessary to go deeper, to attack the system itself. The system that treats women as inferior beings, even in the guise of imbuing them with inestimable worth. As long as the woman is seen as a piece of movable property, as an *inestimable* asset, sought after, possessed, and given, she can still be effectively exploited. It is she whose *so precious* qualities remain instruments of confinement. These feminine qualities justify, within this system, both the gentle caress and the brutal assault, poetic admiration and mistrustful exclusion. Acknowledging this does not mean denying the role played by gallantry in attenuating the level of violence against women.[28] Marriage, which has certainly been by and large an institution of incarceration for women, was also capable of securing their relative emancipation, even in antiquity. Michel Foucault shows this by quoting Greek and Roman authors, first and foremost among them the Stoic philosopher Musonius Rufus, who lived during the first century, under the rule of Nero. In his treatise *On Sexual Indulgence*, Foucault tells us, Musonius Rufus defends the principle of a "symmetrical conjugal fidelity."[29] The medieval Occitan movement of courtly love, or *fin'amor*, with influential patronesses such as Eleanor of Aquitaine in the twelfth century, also did a great deal for the amelioration of women's situation.[30] Without going so far as to claim, with the German sociologist Norbert Elias, that in courtly society, between the fifteenth and the eighteenth centuries in Europe (and particularly in France) "the domination of women by men had been completely abolished,"[31] it is certainly undeniable that, in contrast with the medieval culture of chivalry, women were no longer required to adhere to a strict sexual fidelity. It was certainly thought, in accordance with general opinion, *indelicate* for a husband to forcibly restrain or punish his wife if she fell in love with another man. In the eighteenth century, if sexuality were reduced to the confines of marriage, such an arrangement was even considered vulgar and "bourgeois," unworthy of the nobility. It is true that bourgeois society would in time again proceed to limit sexual freedom, pushing extramarital relationships into the shadows, and reinforcing rules especially to the detriment of women. The process of *modernizing* civilization, and thus substantially improving the condition of women, which began at the end of the fourteenth century—of which the great Italian poet and humanist Petrarch and his deification of the woman he loved was a forerunner—was far from linear. There have been moments of progress followed by movements of regression in terms of sexual freedom and gender equality. We are certainly not proof against any new regression.

It is, in any case, quite clear that women have been more or less capable of effectively gaming and benefiting from the system within which they've been imprisoned for millennia now. The male can be hoisted by his own petard, he can lose at his own game. He can be tripped up in the nets of his own domination. Teetering in precarious balance on the tippy top of his phallus, he can be ably manipulated by women employing the very same charm that was assigned to them by a system he devised in the first place. Yes, women have learned to play men skillfully for their own comfort and survival. They have been able to put to the test the very demands and requirements of virility: stirring jealousy in order to obtain certain benefits, showing off their bodies, while withholding that same body, concealing it even more than is demanded of them. Turning their required effacement into a captivating mystery. But it's still never anything more than a negative, covert power, devoid of any positive recognition. Now, though, it is positive power—no longer dependent on masculine delegation, which goes hand in hand with the full recognition of their will—that they are demanding, without any longer being forced to play on their charms. And they demand that power in terms of actual *fact*, because that power has finally been promised to them by the *law* after more than two centuries of relentless struggle.

THE UNKEPT PROMISE OF MODERNITY

Modernity promised all human beings the same rights in the name of their mere humanity. Still, from the very beginning, women have been excluded. At best, they were confined for their gratification to intellectual salons with no real access to the true bases of constituted power. Eighteenth-century revolutionaries certainly wanted them to rise up in revolt. Women took active roles in all the great European and American democratic revolutions. Promises were even made to them in the thrill of the moment. Nevertheless, the English Bill of Rights of 1689 and the French Declaration of the Rights of Man and of the Citizen of 1789 were limited only to men. One of the earliest feminists in history, Olympe de Gouges, who was equally committed to the abolition of slavery and the fight against racism, drew up in 1791 a *Déclaration des droits de la femme et de la citoyenne* ("Declaration of the Rights of Woman and the Female Citizen"), which was never ratified by the Convention. She demanded nothing more than the application of subjective rights (that is, human rights) to women. She demanded that her sister women be recognized quite simply as citizens, at a time when they were still excluded from the right to own property and the most essential of all civil rights, the right to vote, and were still essentially feudal vassals to men, to fathers, to heads of households, to husbands, and to priests. What good had the French Revolution done them? That was the question that Olympe de Gouges asked. Are women not human beings? Did humanist principles not apply to them as well? The American Declaration of Independence in 1776 stipulates that "all men are created equal." Men, and men alone. The Emancipation Proclamation of 1863 that freed the slaves also said nothing about women. The Fifteenth Amendment to the Constitution of the United States stipulated in 1870 that no person could be refused the right to vote on account of "race, color, or previous condition of servitude."[32] Women remained in a condition of servitude, excluded from basic civil rights, and relegated to a second-class citizenship.

The road since then has been a long one, as, right by right, women have fought to be recognized with a juridical equality that ought to have been part and parcel of the modernity of the Enlightenment. Instead, it took until the twentieth century for them to be given the right to vote. New Zealand was the first democracy to finally extend to them this fundamental civil right, in 1893. Women were given the vote in 1944 in France. But full civil rights still hadn't been acquired. Article 1421 of the French Civil Code, which stated that "the husband alone administers community property" was not repealed until December 23, 1985. The requirement for a young woman's consent to her own marriage was not established until quite late and, until the end of the twentieth century, the concept of rape within marriage was inconceivable. It wasn't until September 5, 1990, that the highest body in the French judiciary, the Court of Cassation, finally recognized the crime of rape between spouses while still married.

Since the turn of the twenty-first century, we might say that we—in the Western democracies—have more or less achieved a 180-degree turn: at last, women are juridically men's equals, after more than two centuries of tireless struggle. More and more women have seized the rights to control their own fates. There are women CEOs, high-level women engineers, women researchers, women authors, and women heads of state. The head of the Pakistani government,

Benazir Bhutto, even chose to remain in power throughout her pregnancy, without the birth of her daughter in January 1990 interfering with her term as prime minister. That was the first time in world history that an acting head of state had given birth (as far as we know). It would not be until 2018 that the young prime minister of New Zealand, Jacinda Ardern, also became pregnant while in office, proving that not only is femininity perfectly compatible with high office, so is maternity.

◈

Nonetheless, men still haven't managed to integrate this reality into their everyday behavior. They still don't quite realize that they can't go on acting the way they used to. A female friend of mine who is an executive confided in me recently that she has a very hard time being taken completely seriously by her coworkers. An assistant to one of her colleagues, and therefore hierarchically her inferior in rank, offhandedly asked her in the middle of a meeting to go and *serve the coffee*. No doubt he thought the discussions underway were too serious and could therefore be of no interest to a woman. This is how men in general still view women, first and foremost as bodies, with all the fantasies of submission those bodies carry in the eyes of men.

THE FALSE AMBIGUITY OF
FEMALE CONSENT

We now come to the heart of the matter: the body. Until the full and thorough recognition of their corporeal sovereignty is attained, women will never concretely be men's equals, not even if they are corporate CEOs or movie superstars. Recognizing this sovereignty is not a matter of eliminating seduction, but rather of escaping from the widespread idea that women don't entirely know what they want. This idea is manifested everywhere: by groups of young men who claim not to have even realized that they were *doing anything wrong* by gang-raping a young woman who was drunk and on drugs, literally dragging her from one place to another in the process, or by the movie scene showing a heroic, manly cowboy with gleaming white teeth forcing a pretty blonde to kiss him.

Raped at age seventeen, the novelist Virginie Despentes writes about how her rapists tried to act as if it wasn't really rape at all, as if she was "just a little slut who didn't know what she wanted, and for whom a little persuading was all that was needed."[33] For years, the novelist never once dared to talk openly about what had happened. Why not? she asked herself. Because she felt humiliated, but above all, ashamed. As if she'd been somehow responsible for what she'd been put through. As if something had been taken from her. But eventually, in time, she came to understand that, if they had denied her will, then they had really taken nothing tangible

72

from her. It was their own fantasy that they had taken from her some part of herself by forcibly penetrating her. She was by no means obliged to adhere to that fantasy. She need not play along with their game of capitalistic virility. No, they had taken nothing from her. Women may have gained rights and standing in the eyes of the law, but they haven't completely defeated the virile fantasy that prevents them from making concrete use of those rights. To recognize their *transcendental subjectivity*, it would first be necessary to deflate that grand illusion.

A woman might want to have a drink with a man. She might want to ask him over to her place in the middle of the night. She might even choose to sleep next to him. She might want to let him caress her, and then stop there. She may choose not to let him penetrate her. And yet, it all seems as if one might both deny the reality of her consent and simultaneously suppose that the slightest sign of positive assent on her part means that she has therefore consented to everything.

It took a long time, as we have seen, for the law to recognize the possibility of rape within marriage. Now, this is the same problem. One may have given one's consent in church or at city hall on such-and-such a date and time. And one may just as well refuse to have sex that very same night. Or else the next day. Or ten years later. Consent is never a blanket, general consent. And it is never definitively acquired, once and for all. But, obviously, as long as one continues to consider, at whatever insidious, unstated level, a woman's body as a form of merchandise, an object of enjoyment (in both senses of enjoying her physically and enjoying her as a civil property) rather than an autonomous subject that can fully enjoy the world (in both senses of enjoying herself physically and enjoying civil rights, among them the right of property), then one will assume that once a transaction has been completed, the *object* does in fact definitively belong to the new proprietor. We've already stated it: in the old days, rape or abduction was sufficient to establish ownership. The owned body, a passive material object, pure capital, cannot express any shift in free will. Such a shift would not be of free will, but simply of a typically feminine fickleness. There's a popular saying for it in French: *"Souvent femme varie"* (Women are often fickle). But if one considers that a woman is a subject with free will, capable of taking pleasure, as is theoretically the case nowadays, then that woman can no longer be the object of any transaction.

The capacity of "modern" men to justify archaic sexual behavior is quite striking. When I was a student at the end of the 1980s, I knew and spent time with a young anarchist. He claimed to be fighting against social inequality; he denounced the sins and ills of capitalism and even the inequality of men and women. But when he was proudly describing to "the guys" his numerous "conquests" as a lady-killer, he completely changed his tone. His favorite expression for a completely successful sexual escapade was: "I totally demolished that girl." He might add: "You can't even begin to imagine what I stuck inside her!" One of his obsessions was sodomizing girls. But only if his "conquest" had never allowed another man to do it to her. To him, the ultimate refinement was to sodomize a married woman who refused (or claimed to refuse) to allow her own husband to engage in that practice. The real pleasure was to send her around the bend for the very first time. One day he chanced to encounter a young woman "who actually liked it," and according to him, that totally took all the fun out of sodomizing her. He thrilled to the excitement of possessing women's bodies, because he firmly believed that they gave themselves to him when he "smashed into them," when he "pounded them," when he "ground away at them," when he "ripped them limb from limb." This attitude makes one think of the men of the Kisii people who live in the south of Kenya, for whom every act of sexual intercourse is a battle against a woman's resistance. A real man ought to be capable of causing pain, humiliating and driving his woman to the brink of tears; for a man, the utmost would be to actually make her cry, in order to prove his mighty power to the rest of the tribe. My anarchist comrade was haunted by only one obsessive fear, that another guy might take pleasure with his wife (because *he* was married, though she, of course, was entirely ignorant of his virile quest for extramarital possession). I doubt that I managed to convince him when I took stands against his behavior and criticized the glaring dissonance between his sexual proclivities and his progressive vision of society.

It is certainly not random that so many progressives, ostensibly advocates of equal rights for women, were implicated in #MeToo scandals, starting with Weinstein himself, a professed Democrat who even helped finance Obama's presidential campaign. Remember also the former president of the French Movement of Young Socialists, an outspoken feminist and yet also a compulsive harasser, discussed earlier in this book. Such has been the case with numerous Hollywood stars, left-leaning artists, and politicians who in theory are feminist and liberal. My hypothesis is that this trend results from the "unbearable" distance between their avowed ideal and the fantasy they continue to harbor of being dominant males. The cognitive dissonance between the progressive social ideas they stand for and their still-patriarchal desire to physically possess women is so disturbing to them, maybe gnawing at them, that some resort to harassment, physical pressure, sexual violence, and even rape. This is further proof that the real issue is now less a question of official rights, of formal equality, than of working to address the innermost fantasy on which gender inequality is primarily based. Without this work, we will continue to turn around the problem, failing to confront it at its disturbing core.

Sexual behavior is necessarily profoundly political, given that women's freedom to enjoy physical satisfaction is at the foundation of the full recognition of their enjoyment of their civil and political rights.

SEX WITHOUT LOVE

In the sexist, macho world, a woman could not possibly have sexual relations without love. A man can, however. Why is that? Because a woman cannot by principle have sex without an emotional relationship. A man can. This idea is yet another way of denying the existence of a female orgasm completely independent of any attachment to the man; hence the taboo and, at the same time, the fascination that still attaches to female masturbation. It is also a way of "proving" that women give themselves body and soul, and therefore deteriorate the state of their *soul* by inflicting wear and tear on their flesh. Many men, even now, in the present day, continue to reproach their girlfriends for their previous use of their own body.

This patriarchal illusion leads us to the highly controversial issue of prostitution. Many people reject prostitution in the name of rejecting the commodification of the body—women's bodies, in particular. The fact that the word *whore* can designate not only a practice, prostitution, but can also be used as an insult meant to devalue a woman who has supposedly slept with "too many" men is quite enlightening. This insult expresses the fury of a man deceived, his current jealousy, or perhaps his retrospective jealousy. It depicts the woman thus described as an object that has been depreciated in proportion to the number of men who have supposedly possessed "it." The fundamental contempt expressed for the prostitute, professional or occasional—sometimes presented as a form of pity—smacks all the same of the capitalist view: she is a passive body being given, and therefore being given away, endlessly degrading itself. A body which can be enjoyed but which can never enjoy.

The problem isn't prostitution itself, but on the one hand sexual slavery, the abject trade in bodies, mistreatment, poverty, disastrous hygienic conditions; and, on the other hand, the humiliating social gaze that imprisons these women in the sexist image of the "whore," the girl without worth because she's already been sold too many times. Aside from that, there is no reason whatsoever to proscribe prostitution as such.

A prostitute doesn't actually sell her body. She performs a sexual service. She might just as well be giving a massage. But we are still influenced by the prejudice that a woman who sleeps with a man can't help but *lose* a part of herself. Likewise, she can't possibly have sexual relations without her feelings being engaged. This, at least, once again, is what many men choose to believe. This vision of a woman who cannot accept sex without love—not, that is, unless she's a "slut" (or a witch or a hysteric), in other words, an unnatural being (which might be tantamount to a "whore")—is a pure and unadulterated creation of virility. The research of the Finnish sociologist and feminist Anna Kontula shows that prostitution can be sexually fulfilling for women if social conditions are favorable:[34] provided the woman practicing prostitution is protected, with the status of a self-employed professional, able to pick and choose her clients, as may well be the case in Finland, and also is socially respected. In the same sense, the prominent writer Catherine Millet described how she used to go to the Bois de Boulogne to offer sexual services free of charge to immigrants in a state of considerable economic and sexual deprivation, and that she felt by no means morally degraded by the experience. She even went on to say, somewhat mischievously, that this was no doubt thanks to her good Christian upbringing, which taught her to always consider that the body and the soul are two entirely separate things.

As with prostitution, social attitudes toward rape serve to comfort and confirm male domination. We must abandon once and for all the virile fiction of the sheer degradation of the female body that has supposedly been *possessed* by a rapist. A fiction, moreover, that helps to fuel the victim's sense of shame, so that she now feels twice raped. First of all, of course, by her rapist, but after that by the distasteful gaze that society at large turns upon her. And with society, the judicial system. The author Catherine Millet shocked many readers by tossing out the statement that rape is no worse, in principle, than any other form of physical assault. In my reading of her declaration, she wasn't saying that rape isn't serious, but rather that it was important not to fall into the patriarchal trap that entails a double punishment for the victim. The seriousness of rape is strictly bound up with its transgression against the free will of another person, on the one hand, while that seriousness is, on the other hand, proportional to the physical and psychological damage suffered. No more and no less. It is neither an indelible defilement, nor a divine punishment, much less an irremediable depredation.

That is also what Virginie Despentes is trying to say about her own rape. In the movie she made, based on her book, *Baise-moi (Rape Me)*,[35] two young women are attacked by two men who take them to a deserted warehouse to rape them. One of the girls fights back, screams, and begs for mercy. She is beaten bloody by the men, overexcited by the resistance she's putting up. The other girl, with a disdainful glance, obeys every last instruction, and winds up "disabling" her rapist by deflating his fantasy of possessing her. After the two men leave, the first girl sobs in despair: "How could you let them do that to you?" The second girl responds coldly: "I don't give a fuck about their pussy-assed dicks"; and then she adds: "Sweetie pie, I can't keep fuckwads like them from getting in, so I just don't leave any valuables lying around in there."

Men have been transacting with, trading, abducting, and raping women, at least since the Neolithic. Never the other way around. But it doesn't have to be that way. And, for that matter, it is not only outsiders, foreign enemies, who attack women. According to the World Health Organization (WHO), around the world, nearly a third of women who have been in a relationship report that they have experienced some form of physical and/or sexual violence by their intimate partner.

GENDER MALAISE

The system of virility, which engendered, as we have seen, the archaic understanding of femininity, is breathing its last. But in the meantime, it still lives and, in its death throes, continues to do enormous harm. A great disarray reigns over the surviving patriarchal civilization. Changes in behavior have occurred precipitously among the younger generations, especially among young women, but at the same time there are still sizable numbers of other individuals, especially men, who cling to the old system, and who are deeply disoriented. This is the same sense of disarray that, in the television series *Masters of Sex*, has taken hold of the young, attractive, and likable medical intern, eager and full of good intentions, who falls head over heels in love with his boss's assistant, none other than Virginia Johnson, cofounder of modern sexology. What's more, Virginia Johnson is a sort of UFO, entirely independent, free in both her emotional and her sexual lives, living in the midst of the profoundly chauvinist and sexist society of America in the late 1950s.

Two scenes from the first episode of the series offer a concentrate of the essential malaise that still afflicts us today. Here is the first scene. The intern and Virginia Johnson have just eaten dinner together for the first time. He takes her home. They're at her doorstep, and he pushes gently to come inside and have one last drink. Recognizing his intention, she makes it clear to him that she isn't ready to make an emotional investment with anyone at this point in her life. She adds, however, that she would very much like to be friends with him. He beats a dispirited retreat, admitting to her that he'd thought of kissing her the whole drive over to her place from the restaurant. She smiles at him and tells him that she'd be glad to kiss him; but, she adds, only if they can remain friends. The young intern, a handsome hunk with a bright future, in the heat of the virile chase, can't quite wrap his head around this. Immediately afterward, they're in bed having sex. And they start having enthusiastic sex on a regular basis after that. As a general rule, she asks him to leave before dawn. He doesn't understand the reason for this. She initiates him into the world of feminine pleasure while offering him sexual delights he'd never imagined in his wildest dreams. He falls madly in love with her. But she doesn't fall in love with him. He asks her to marry him. She turns him down, with great kindness. He is rocked to his foundations.

In the second scene, crucial in my view, his rage bursts forth in the middle of a party. Virginia doesn't wish to be seen with him, because as far as she's concerned, they're not a couple. He shouts at her: "How many times have you let me fuck you? Answer me!" and, increasingly scandalized, he points out "I have been in your bed. I have been inside you." She replies, still very gently: "You are my friend. I care about you very much." He can't take anymore, at this point he bursts out: "You'll let me do anything, everything to you." To which she responds with disarming simplicity: "It's because I like it, because you like it." This time, he can't contain his violence any longer and he slaps her, while hissing at her with despairing vehemence: "Wear the lab coat, Virginia. Run the study. Play doctor all you want. At the end of the day, all you really are is a whore!"

More and more women resemble Virginia Johnson. And we should certainly recognize that a fair number of men, without necessarily being awful alpha males, increasingly resemble that disappointed medical intern. Those men simply no longer know what to do with their virility. They don't know where to put it, or how to behave appropriately. They don't even know, in some cases, how they should feel in the face of this newly won female liberty. They may feel powerless, a feeling that intensifies until it culminates in an insult: "At the end of the day, all you really are is a whore!" You cling to what you know. There is unquestionably a civil war underway between archaic man and modern man. The modern man recognizes the existence of women's pleasure and, therefore, their free will, so to speak—their capacity to enjoy themselves and the world thoroughly. The struggle subsists in the growing competition, since the middle of the decade of the aughts, between two models: virile pornography (even more extreme than before) and a new feminine eroticism. The former model remains entirely under the mental grip of the capitalization of women's bodies from every angle, to the verge of utter absurdity: women are shown on their knees, sprawled out, penetrated in every orifice, grasped, literally "disassembled" in front of the camera lens, while being drawn and quartered, insulted by men with big muscles, and sprayed with multidirectional ejaculations. This is the notorious woman's body, desirable because it is diminished, punished, and vanquished. It is a recapitulation of such archaic practices of punishment as those found among the Cheyenne Native Americans, where a man whose wife had cheated on him could invite all the single men in the tribe to punish his spouse by gang-raping her. We can also find it in the pornographic practice of *bukkake*, a Japanese word originally, in which men ejaculate collectively onto the submissive face of a woman who takes it, obediently and thoroughly defiled. It's a model of desperate and despairing sexuality because, in its complacent contemplation of an imaginary war and vengeance without a cause, and therefore never slaked, it does nothing but endlessly stoke men's feelings of impotence. In the final analysis, this model does far more damage to men than to women. This pornography still survives in slightly seedy shops with tinted plate-glass windows while it also proliferates on the Internet, reaching an ever-growing and ever-younger audience.

The latter model emphasizes female desire and pleasure and its right to independence and autonomy, and it translates, for instance, into the emergence, development, and staggering diversification of the market for sex toys. The sex toy designed for women has become a potential gift any loving man might want to give his partner. It will come boxed and wrapped in luxurious packaging reminiscent of the aesthetic of perfume or jewelry. It can be purchased and unwrapped in broad daylight. This is no longer a diminishment of femininity, but rather a brand-new game being played. A mutual, reciprocal game. A game played on equal terms by both parties, that involves both players equally, no longer a unilateral simulacrum of the hunt. Not all women are entirely at ease with the new world looming on the horizon. In some cases, they aren't ready to abandon their old impulses and reflexes. They may be attached to old-school femininity, clinging to a belittling, sexual domination, the silence of timidity, one-sided modesty, and a comfortable state of dependency; in other words, the Eternal Feminine, itself nothing more than a projection of virility.

However much the world may have changed, the majority of men still cling to their time-honored privileges. Inequality in terms of housework, for instance, is still unmistakable. Men's refusal to release their death grip is even more clearly expressed in their patriarchal reaction to the feminine orgasm. They started by denying its existence. Then they did their best to suppress it. Nowadays, any man who claims to be modern—who is actually an updated, latter-day macho man—will attempt to appropriate it for himself, instead. Mockingly, he boasts that he can make his female partner come like no one else. He is thus able to continue *believing* that he possesses her thanks to the orgasm that he *believes* he alone is able to give her. It's time to be done, once and for all, with this last, lingering virile illusion.

DON'T FEAR THE FREEDOM

Donald Trump has become the living symbol of the roaring resistance of the archaic male: according to his former adviser Stephen K. Bannon, he is "maybe the last of the alpha males." One of his greatest pleasures, by his own admission, is to sleep with his friends' wives.[36] Trump is possessed by his own thirst for possession. He hunts for a trophy woman, a *woman as capital* at the highest possible market price, in order to be able to show her off: the youngest, the prettiest, the blondest, the most submissive. This married couple that brings together a lecherous old billionaire, fairly bursting with virility, and a much younger Slovenian model, Melania, fairly bursting with femininity, is emblematic of the old world. Trump personifies the last-ditch defense of the supposedly scorned and flouted power of the American people who, through him, are finally able to get even. Hence the popularity of the utterly virile slogan: *Make America Great Again*. The president's outrageous machismo can be found at work in his conceptions of the economy, international relations, and law: take, increase, measure against, build a great wall, reject all relations. In a sense, it's the swan song of the patriarchy. But it's a swan song that may drag on for some time.

A different world can be glimpsed in the figure of the young President Emmanuel Macron. As a married couple, Emmanuel and Brigitte Macron have turned upside-down all the old patriarchal codes of conduct. A young man, seductive, cultivated, ambitious, and with a brilliant future ahead of him falls head-over-heels in love with a woman much older than him and marries her. What's more, she is an active, ambitious woman, divorced and independent. She is the polar opposite of archaic femininity, just as her husband is the polar opposite of archaic masculinity. A male who has also transcended the desire for any direct offspring, all the while acting as the adoptive father of his wife's children. Then, once he had ascended to the summit of governmental power, this new French president apparently felt no need to find a younger woman, as certain of his older colleagues had done, in a transparent bid to affirm their virility. This unorthodox series of personal decisions naturally led to his being suspected of homosexuality and bisexuality, much like what happened to the proverbial high school boy who, in the courtyard of the school, because he refused to hunt and chase girls, was also suspected of femininity, of being a little "girly."

Might we just as well say that this first lady isn't feminine? No, far from it. Might we also say that this French president isn't virile? No, absolutely not. If anything, he seems rather authoritarian. Zeus-like, as the journalists like to write. All the same, this couple has been able to shock, question, and surprise as if they were somehow exceptional, provocative, so utterly at odds with the millennial norms of sexual capitalism. As a couple, at any rate, they offer a case study, by their mere existence, of an unprecedented cultural mutation in which the feminine and the masculine can persist, while redeploying themselves in a liberated fashion.

One sometimes has the feeling, at the point we've come to, that there are only two possible orientations: the preservation of a steadily fading old-school patriarchal world, with the Trumps, man and wife, or personalities like Harvey Weinstein, as some of its most remarkable specimens. Or else the wholesale abolition of virility and its negative corollary, femininity. As long as patriarchal domination remains the implicit norm, men and women will remain in part prisoners of their quondam roles. And so they hardly seem, all things considered, to have any alternative but a radical revolt or a reactionary defense of the old world. I believe, however, that the old world is already condemned and that gendered and sexual relations are in the process of being concretely redesigned, above and beyond that alternative.

Let's take just one example: Internet dating platforms such as Tinder have largely rendered obsolete the old methods of masculine control over women's bodies. Any woman at all—and likewise, any man at all—can nowadays discreetly and immediately satisfy their sexual desires by means of their phones. Without risk. Without an intermediary. Some observers say that this is crass commodification of sex. I don't believe them one bit. Clearly, that's more upsetting to men than to women, who suddenly have access to a way of life once considered essentially masculine. Out of manly control, they are taking part in a game that has suddenly become reciprocal and egalitarian. In contemporary couples, both partners know perfectly well, man as well as woman, that they can easily satisfy their sexual desires elsewhere. Thereafter the satisfaction of their sexual needs can no longer constitute the sole engine driving their relationship. They need to keep things fresh. There are new and greater reciprocal demands. In a way, partners must show themselves to be mutually more attentive to the quality of their sexual interactions.

PLAYING WITH OUR DIFFERENCES

Does this new world, still in a state of gestation, necessarily have to culminate in the abolition of gender distinctions, the effacement of virility and femininity? Certainly, femininity established itself in the wake of virility. Nevertheless, even if it is a clear testimonial to a tradition of masculine domination, femininity—as much as masculinity—has become a culture with its own remarkable achievements. To make a tabula rasa—a clean slate—of it would be comparable to a situation in which African Americans suddenly decided to refuse to speak English, replacing it with a new idiom created out of whole cloth, on the pretext that English was the language under which they had been reduced to slavery. They would thus be abolishing their memory as a group, including all memory of the revolt that made them what they are today: free people. In actual fact, they simply reappropriated, subverted, and changed the language of their oppressor, to such an extent that it has become a tool of their emancipation. As a result, a rich and distinctively African American poetry, literature, music, and art continually shape American culture. The same is true of the former francophone colonies. That is the way we must understand the Algerian author Kateb Yacine when he writes that "the French language is our spoils of war." In the same way, rather than trying to delete it, we should work to reappropriate, subvert, and change the meaning of the distinction between the feminine and the masculine.

Dominant virility was born of men's feelings of impotence in the face of the fantasy of women's overwhelming force. They therefore imposed upon women an undervalued identity and the cult of the very phallus that they pretended women *lacked*; a lack that made them less-than *by their very nature.* Girls' so-called penis envy, their supposedly missing phallus, was therefore nothing more than an imaginary by-product of the male feelings of impotence. In spite of that, the brutal and forcible suppression of sexual differences based upon multiple millennia of life in common, on however unequal a basis, strikes me as neither possible nor advisable. Millions of men and women would feel they had been deprived of their fantasies. And they would feel guilty for the fact that they continue to cherish them. Encouraging genuine equality, from kindergarten to the workplace, would be enough to create a space where our fantasies could be rebuilt on new foundations. Whether you like it or not, our shared history has created shared desires to which we cannot help but feel a certain attachment. A female friend of mine told me recently: "I feel deeply that I am a feminist, but I am not ready to give up my femininity. I like to use makeup, I like long dresses and stiletto heels." What is at stake is to be able to experience a new femininity, independent of the imperium of virility. And, contrariwise, a masculinity that recognizes female desire and pleasure, women's positive enjoyment of the world, and is therefore not patriarchal. Of which, it strikes me, the Macrons as a couple offer an excellent testimonial, as do millions of other less famous couples.

It's all a matter of the fluidity of the fantasies and games shared. Nothing keeps us from playing at being a sexual dominator or, the other way around, from acting out submissive fragility. These roles do not need to be fixed and characterized, destined to imprison the genders in a hierarchical order; claiming to represent *natural* types. The slogan might be: Let us differentiate ourselves without discriminating. Let us seek reciprocity. That would allow us, in accordance with the Nietzschean expression, to *transvalue* the meaning of femininity, as well as that of virility, and therefore to transvalue the dynamic of human relations. In contrast with the more banal transformation that changes forms, transvaluation *keeps* existing forms, but *reverses*, or more accurately opens up their value. The shift in meaning of stiletto heels illustrates this potential transvaluation, which is already at work in certain domains. In the old days, those shoes could only form part of the panoply of the skinny, frail woman, timidly perched upon them, precariously balanced. Now plenty of women in upper management—CEOs, lawyers, and others still—have reappropriated stiletto heels. A woman like this imposes a sense of seriousness and hauteur on everything feminine: she is a woman solidly planted on her heels, who knows what she's talking about and what she wants.

Meaning won't stand still. Others can wear corsets. Or they can choose not to wear bras, as they prefer. And assign to them whatever meaning they wish. Wearing a corset if you aren't obliged to wear it, in a world where the principle of masculine domination no longer has any currency, becomes a form of freedom. Just as wearing a Muslim hijab in the United States might be a sign of freedom, whereas wearing it in Saudi Arabia has by no means anything like the same significance. But the necessary prior condition for the transvaluation of femininity, that is to say, its free reappropriation, is the full recognition of women's free will. As long as Weinstein and his ilk are tolerated at the helm of society, the new femininity, freely undertaken and fully autonomous, exactly like the new masculinity, can never be fully deployed.

TOWARD PEACE BETWEEN THE GENDERS

The distinction between feminine and masculine is, theoretically at least, less and less firmly fixed, including when it comes to their respective physical performance. Generally speaking, women nowadays are catching up with men in most sports. This is true not only in those sports thought to lend themselves to women's feminine faculties of dexterity such as fencing, but also in disciplines requiring brute force, such as the shot put or the javelin toss; and even in other, more sinewy and muscular athletic events such as the high jump; and in contests challenging in cardiac and pulmonary terms, such as foot races or sprints. According to the social scientist Catherine Louveau, who studies the evolution of sports performance, the way things are going now, she would not rule out the possibility that women will catch up with men within a few decades. That will be part of rendering obsolete—even further *transvaluating*—the virilizing initiatic aspect of sports. For the moment, however, the chief obstacle to women's catching up with men seems to be more psychological than physical. Many high-level athletes have the impression that they lose their femininity as they triumph in competition. As they develop their musculature, their bone structure, their pulmonary capacity, they supposedly thereby lose the delicacy that is the essence of feminine charm. They are afraid that they will no longer be desirable, because they have become excessively virilized. Don't we refer to some of them as somewhat mannish, after all! Until 1968 athletes were forced to pass gynecological and morphological tests to make sure they were "real women." If they failed, they were ruled out of competition. And genetic testing is still done in sports to ensure the femininity of women athletes.[37] For that matter, starting from the earliest childhood, isn't a girl who's stronger and more brazen than the average often called a "tomboy"?

We can observe the same phenomenon of malaise in certain women who occupy dominant social positions, who seem to have it all. Women who are no longer forced to engage in transactional dealings with their bodies in return for a status conferred by a man. There are women who are expressing an open-minded and joyful sexuality, but who often feel frustrated because they are unable to form an enduring couple. They despair at ever being able to find a stable family situation, as if some curse were weighing down upon them. They are viewed as castrating bitches by many men, stripped bare in their feelings of impotence. Simone de Beauvoir wrote that, in the war between the sexes, one cannot help but be one enemy's accomplice. No doubt this millennia-old complicity may also be brought to bear on behalf of an egalitarian peace between the sexes.

EPILOGUE: TRANSVALUATION

How can we avoid slipping directly from repression to depression? Many of my fellow men feel unmanned in the presence of a sexually and financially independent woman. The longtime driving forces of their virility no longer work. They might therefore take umbrage and simmer in the doldrums of resentment, or even violence. They need to let go of that resentment. Really and truly. We must stop assigning preconceived roles to ourselves and to others. And stop assigning equally preconceived identities. Not the identity of the childbearing mother. Not the identity of the Barbie doll. Nor that of the hero. Nor that of *the one who knows*. Much less the identity of the lady-killer. No predetermined identities at all. We should strive to make situations more fluid. We can't calcify on a fixed image of the man we are supposed to be, and especially, *appear* to be. We must overcome whatever shame or embarrassment might arise on a date or in a relationship with a woman who earns more than us, is more successful, occupies a more elevated hierarchical role, or enjoys a more thriving and fulfilling sex life. None of that means we shouldn't engage in seduction. We can play along with the other's consent, whether that's in search of one-night stands or the love of a lifetime. It doesn't really matter. We must no longer see the woman as a target to hit, an object to take possession of, an opportunity for a show of force, but instead as a subject with a will of their own, and desirable precisely because any and all interactions are voluntary. Women are by no means less than we are if they act as freely as we do. Equality is liberating because it reveals the contrivances of the social theater that once imposed upon us, the men as well as the women, roles written in advance. We therefore create a space of trust in ourselves and our fellow humans, like some unexplored land where something new and shared can be built.

But in order to be capable of such a transvaluation, we must first free ourselves of the pornographic onanism haunted by castration anxiety. We can no longer use women's bodies to reassure ourselves. We must mature with them instead of trying to use them to mature, by degrading them physically and symbolically. Stop holding them hostage for our frustrations. Live with them in a state of interdependence, without dependency. We would benefit immensely from all that.

Archaic men focused on the mastery of the *other* while blinding themselves with the fantasy of the transcendence of the *self*. Contrariwise, transvalued virility would focus on the mastery of the *self* while respecting the transcendence of the *other*. I accept that the nature of the other, in its very singularity, eludes my understanding. I no longer have any need, a priori, inasmuch as I am a man, to prove my worth, or even my love, through my sexual, economic, or professional performance. But I also accept, reciprocally, that women no longer have any need, a priori, to prove their worth, or even their love, through their fawning admiration, the bestowal of their body, or the abandonment of their ambitions, much less than by their submission. The man can thus sidestep the need for a virile performance (earn more money, withhold an orgasm or give one) and the expectations of the feminine offering (bodily abnegation and docile admiration). Roles, emotions, and identities, then, can be redefined, though never definitively, and with neither prejudice nor frustration: in a couple, having children or not, mixed paternity and maternity, working together, desiring and loving the freedom of the other partner in trivial everyday matters and in the larger existential orientations; and, in general, whether as a single or a couple, experiencing the sexual exchange as a reciprocal matter, sharing mutually selected fantasies, whether that's in the context of a short-term fling or a long-term relationship. A new type of solidarity could thus be constructed between the genders. A new form of trust. A new and intimate social contract. A new and shared transcendence. But there is no way we can hope to achieve such a revolution in awareness without thinking against ourselves, as is the case with racism. And, as with racism, we'll never succeed unless we radically reshape the education and upbringing of our children.

As I wrote at the beginning of this book, I was expressing myself in response to my initial doubts and concerns, from my own troubled conscience. I haven't written about women as such, but rather about the femininity constructed by that castrating, Weinsteinian masculinity that still remains dominant. Above and beyond the transvaluation of the meanings of the feminine and the masculine, it is the fluidity of genders and desires that is in play nowadays, along with the opportunity for a new exploration of self in the context of human relations. I don't believe that we need fear this new freedom;

if anything, we should fear those who wish to forcibly protect us from a future that they consider too uncertain and chaotic. The achievement of modernity would be the promise finally kept of a world in which all ways of being can coexist, without discrimination, and therefore, it goes without saying, without the most archaic form of discrimination—the most durable, general, and stubbornly resistant form in all humanity. Because "the tie that binds her to her oppressors is unlike any other,"[38] as Simone de Beauvoir wrote in 1949, women had not yet succeeded in saying "we" in order to rise up against the discrimination that oppresses them. This is no longer true, given that millions of women have dared to say #MeToo, and that the echoes of their words continue to resonate, in unison, from one end of the planet to the other.

ENDNOTES

1. Michael Wolff, *Fire and Fury. Inside the Trump White House* (Henry Holt and Company, 2018), 27.

2. "How Tough Is It to Change a Culture of Harassment? Ask Women at Ford," *The New York Times*, 19 December 2017.

3. "Nous défendons une liberté d'importuner, indispensable à la liberté sexuelle», *Le Monde*, 9 January 2018.

4. Emmanuel Kant, *La Fausse Subtilité des quatre figures du syllogisme*, 1762, §6 (Œuvres Philosophiques, t. I, Paris, Gallimard), 193.

5. *Id. Sur la question mise au concours par l'Académie royale des sciences pour l'année 1791: quels sont les progrès réels de la métaphysique en Allemagne depuis le temps de Leibniz et de Wolff*, 1791, Première Section (Œuvres philosophiques, t. III, Paris, Gallimard, 1986), 1225.

6. *Id. Sur le lieu commun: il se peut que cela soit juste en théorie, mais, en pratique, cela ne vaut rien*, 1793, II (Œuvres philosophiques, t. III, Paris, Gallimard, 1986), 270.

7. Emmanuel Kant, *An Answer to the Question: 'What Is Enlightenment?'* trans. H. B. Nisbet (Penguin Books, 2009).

8. Marshall Sahlins, *Stone Age Economics* (New York: de Gruyter, 1972).

9. Christine Delphy, *L'Ennemi principal* (Paris, Syllepse, 2013).

10. Françoise Héritier, *Masculin/Féminin. La pensée de la différence* (Paris, Odile Jacob, 2012), 213.

11. Peggy Reeves Sanday, "Rape-free versus rape-prone: How culture makes a difference," *Evolution, gender, and rape*, 2003.

12. Youssef Courbage, Emmanuel Todd, *Le Rendez-vous des civilisations* (Paris, Seuil, 2007), 63.

13. Julien Gracq, *The Castle of Argol*, trans. Louise Varese (Pushkin Press, 1999), 58.

14. *Ibid.*, 59.

15. *Ibid.*, 60.

16. Simone de Beauvoir, *The Second Sex*, trans. Constance Borde and Sheila Malovany-Chevallier (Vintage, 2011), 386.

17. *Ibid.*, 283.

18. Aristotle, *Generation of Animals*, trans. A. L. Peck (Cambridge: Harvard University Press, 1942).

19. Plato, *Timaeus*, trans. Benjamin Jowett, classics.mit.edu/Plato/timaeus.html.

20. Priscilla Touraille, *Hommes grands, women petites. Une évolution coûteuse. Les régimes de genre comme force sélective de l'adaptation biologique* (Paris, Éditions de la Maison des Sciences de l'Homme, 2008).

21. Sylvie Chaperon, "Organes sexuels," *Encyclopédie critique du genre* (Paris, La Découverte, 2016), 428–438.

22. Pierre Noailles, "Les tabous du mariage dans le droit religieux primitif des romains," *Revue des études latines*, 1935, 27.

23. Anne Chapman, *Drama and Power in a Hunting Society. The Selk'nam of Tierra del Fuego* (Cambridge University Press, 1982).

24. *La Possession de Loudun. Textes choisis et présentés par Michel de Certeau* (Paris, Julliard, 1978).

25. George Sand, *Story of My Life: The Autobiography of George Sand*, ed. Thelma Jurgrau, SUNY series, Women Writers in Translation (Albany, NY: SUNY Press), 456.

26. Virginia Woolf, *A Room of One's Own* (London, The Hogarth Press, 1929).

27. Jacques G. Ruelland, *L'Empire des gènes. L'histoire de la socio-biologie* (Lyon, ENS Éditions, 2004).

28. Norbert Elias, *The Civilizing Process: Sociogenetic and Psychogenetic Investigations,* revised edition, eds. Eric Dunning, Johan Goudsblom, Stephen Mennell; trans. Edmund Jephcott (Blackwell Publishers, 2000).

29. Michel Foucault, *The History of Sexuality, Vol. 3: The Care of the Self,* trans. Robert Hurley (New York: Vintage Books, 1988), 172.

30. Denis de Rougemont, *Love in the Western World,* trans. Montgomery Belgion (Princeton University Press, 1983).

31. Norbert Elias, *The Civilizing Process.*

32. *"The right of citizens of the United States to vote shall not be denied or abridged by the United States or by any state on account of race, color, or previous condition of servitude."*

33. Virginie Despentes and Stéphanie Benson, *King Kong Theory* (The Feminist Press at the City University of New York, 2010), 34.

34. Anna Kontula, "The Sex Worker and Her Pleasure," *Current Sociology,* vol. 56, issue 4, July 2008, 605–620.

35. Published in English as *Rape Me,* the French *Baise-moi* literally translates as "Fuck Me."

36. Michael Wolff, *Fire and Fury, op. cit.,* 32. *"For Steve Bannon, Trump's unique political virtue was as an alpha male, maybe the last of the alpha males. A 1950s man, a Rat Pack type, a character out of Mad Men,"* 33.

37. Anaïs Bohuon, *Test de fémininité dans les compétitions sportives. Une histoire classée X* (Paris, Éditions IXe, 2012).

38. de Beauvoir, *The Second Sex.*